Writing The Psychology Paper

Robert J. Sternberg
Yale University

BARRON'S EDUCATIONAL SERIES, INC.
Woodbury, New York • London • Toronto

Acknowledgements

I am indebted to several people for their assistance with this book. Tom Trabasso provided a careful and detailed critique that greatly enhanced the quality of the final product. Michael Kubovy, Miriam Schustack, Betty Sternberg, and Allan Wagner also provided helpful advice. Ella Futrell typed the manuscript. The American Psychological Association graciously permitted me to summarize the APA *Publication Manual*, Second Edition, in Chapter 6. Finally, my mentors, Gordon Bower and Endel Tulving, served as model writers for me to emulate. I thank them all.

All inquiries should be addressed to:
Barron's Educational Series, Inc.
113 Crossways Park Drive
Woodbury, New York 11797

Library of Congress Catalog Card No. 77-9250

International Standard Book No. 0-8120-0772-7

Library of Congress Cataloging in Publication Data
Sternberg, Robert J
  Writing the psychology paper.
  Includes bibliographical references.
  1. Report writing.   2. Psychological literature.
I. Title.
BF76.8.S73   808'.066'15021   77-9250
ISBN 0-8120-0772-7

PRINTED IN THE UNITED STATES OF AMERICA

67   510   987

Table of Contents

Acknowledgements   II
Introduction   V

CHAPTER

1   **Eight Common Misconceptions
    about Psychology Papers**   1

2   **Steps in Writing the Library Research Paper**   19
    Deciding upon a Topic for a Paper   19
    Searching the Literature   23
    Preparing an Outline   28
    Writing the Paper   36

3   **Steps in Writing the
    Experimental Research Paper**   39
    Planning Experimental Research   39
    Executing Experimental Research   60
    Analyzing Data from Experimental Research   61
    Reporting Experimental Research   62

4   **Rules for Writing the Psychology Paper**   77

5   **Commonly Misused Words**   93
    Nontechnical Terms   93
    Technical Terms   103

6 American Psychological Association Guidelines for Psychology Papers   121

Typing the Paper   121
Grammar   123
Headings   136
Quantitative Issues   137
References   143
Reference Notes   146
Footnotes   148
Tables   150
Figures   155
A Final Word   157

7 References for the Psychology Paper   159

General References   160
Journal References   166

8 Standards for Evaluating the Psychology Paper   189

Synopses of Four Psychology Papers   191
Eight Standards for Evaluating the Contribution to Knowledge of Psychology Papers   205

9 Submitting a Paper to a Journal   213

Deciding upon a Journal   213
Submitting the Paper   215
The Editorial Decision   216
The Aftermath   217

References   219

Appendix: A Sample Paper Typed According to APA Guidelines   223

Index   244

Introduction

Most undergraduate and graduate students of psychology receive little or no formal training in writing the psychology paper. It is commonly believed that students receive sufficient training through informal channels, and so will acquire the necessary skills on their own. The conventional psychology curriculum provides evidence that this belief is widespread. Whereas almost all psychology departments offer courses in how to design experiments and analyze experimental results, very few departments offer courses in how to report experiments. Although some departments include this topic as part of another course, even this modest amount of training appears to be rare.

Do students learn to write psychology papers on their own? My experience reading psychology papers suggests that they do not. Moreover, this experience is shared by other psychology professors, and by professors in other disciplines as well. One of the most common topics of conversation today is the inadequacy of students' writing. But since we do not give students adequate training, we have ourselves to blame.

The purpose of this book is to provide the basic information students need to write psychology papers. This information is contained in nine chapters. Although the chapters were intended to be read in the order in which they are presented, they are for the most part self-contained, and hence can be read in almost any order.

Chapter 1 presents and discusses eight common misconceptions that students hold about psychology papers. I have found that many of these misconceptions are reinforced rather than extinguished by conventional academic training. Most students come to believe, for example, that journal articles are and should be autobiographical—that the logical development of ideas in a psychology paper reflects their historical development in the psychologist's head. Accepting this notion as a presupposition, the students often believe that authors of journal articles can plan their research and predict their findings well in advance, often down to the last detail. Professional psychologists know better, and students will also know better after they read Chapter 1.

Chapters 2 and 3 present the sequence of steps psychologists follow in writing papers. Chapter 2 deals with library research papers, Chapter 3 with experimental research papers. The sequence of steps begins with the search for ideas and ends with the publication of a finished paper. Many students have only a fuzzy idea of the sequence of steps and of how this sequence is presented to the reader of a psychology paper. Consider two examples. First, would the procedure by which subjects are assigned to treatment groups be described more appropriately in the *Procedure* or in the *Design* section of a psychology paper? Second, is the extensive use of tables and figures to clarify the presentation of experimental data encouraged or discouraged in journal articles? The answer to the first question is *Design;* the answer to the second question is *discouraged.*

Chapter 4 contains rules for writing psychology papers. The rules are ones that most students have learned but few students follow. One of the reasons students fail to follow these rules is that they forget what they are. The chances are good that you remember learning something about avoiding "dangling constructions," but that you either don't look for dangling constructions in your writing or you don't even remember exactly what a dangling construction is. Chapter 4 will remind you about dangling constructions and other pitfalls in writing papers.

Chapter 5 contains a list of commonly misused words and describes the proper usage of each of these words. The meanings of these words, like the rules of writing, are quickly learned but quickly forgotten early in one's career as a student. For example, probably fewer than 10% of the papers (that, which) are published in psychological journals consistently use the relative pronouns *that* and *which* correctly. (While, Although) these papers are certainly publishable, their readability would be enhanced by proper English usage. Which word belongs in place of each parenthesized expression? In the first sentence, the proper word is *that;* in the second sentence, the proper word is *Although*.

Chapter 6 summarizes the American Psychological Association guidelines for writing psychology papers. Regardless of how well you write, you must learn a number of rules that are specific to the writing of psychology papers. Different disciplines follow different guidelines for writing, and one is expected to write according to the guidelines of the appropriate discipline. A common mistake occurs when students follow Modern Language Association guidelines, which are the ones most students learn in high school. Although these guidelines are appropriate for writing in the humanities, they are not appropriate for writing in psychology. Test yourself. Does one abbreviate centimeters as *cm* or *cm.?* Does one abbreviate feet as *ft* or *ft.?* Does one test *10* subjects or *ten* subjects? Does one test *8* subjects or *eight* subjects? The rules of the American Psychological Association lead to answers of *cm, ft., 10,* and *eight*. The rules of the Modern Language Association lead to answers of *cm., ft., ten,* and *eight*. Learning to write a psychology paper involves learning certain rules that are unique to writing psychology papers.

Chapter 7 contains a list and description of many of the

references that psychologists use when writing psychology papers. The list includes both general references and journals. Familiarity with these references can save enormous amounts of time. Suppose, for example, that you are writing a paper in which your main thesis is that the work of Julius Schnitzelbonk has been undervalued in the psychological literature. To what source could you turn for a virtually complete listing of citations to the work of Schnitzelbonk, or of anyone else, for that matter? The answer is the *Social Science Citation Index*. This and other valuable references are described in Chapter 7.

Chapter 8 deals with the criteria psychologists use to evaluate the contribution to knowledge of psychology papers. What characteristics distinguish truly exceptional psychology papers from good ones, and good ones from poor ones? Why do some papers continue to have an impact upon the field long after other papers have been forgotten? Chapter 8 addresses these questions.

Chapter 9 contains practical suggestions for submitting a psychology paper to a professional journal. What considerations enter into the choice of a journal? What happens to a paper once it is submitted? What are the possible courses of action a journal editor can take? You will find out when you read Chapter 9.

The Appendix contains a sample paper typed according to APA guidelines. The paper is presented as it was typed, rather than as it would be presented in a journal. The paper illustrates many of the principles described in Chapter 6.

As you learn more and more about psychology, you will discover that writing for an audience of psychologists requires a unique set of skills. For most students, merely reading and writing psychology papers is insufficient to acquire these skills. This book is intended for and dedicated to these students.

CHAPTER 1

Eight Common Misconceptions about Psychology Papers

Misconception #1: *Writing the psychology paper is the most routine, least creative aspect of the scientific enterprise, requiring much time but little imagination.*

Many students lose interest in their research projects as soon as the time comes to write about them. Their interest is in planning for and making new discoveries, not in communicating their discoveries to others. A widely believed fallacy underlies their attitude. The fallacy is that the discovery process ends when the communication process begins. Although the major purpose of writing a paper is to communicate your thoughts to others, another important purpose is to help you form and organize your thoughts.

Reporting your findings in writing requires you to commit yourself to those findings and to your interpretation of them, and opens you to criticism (as well as praise) from others. It is perhaps for this reason as much as any other that many students are reluctant to report their research. But the finality of a written report also serves as a powerful incentive to do your best thinking, and to continue thinking as you write your paper. It requires you to tie up the loose ends that you might otherwise have left untied. As a result, reporting your findings presents just as much of a challenge as planning the research and analyses that led to those findings.

I have often thought I knew what I wanted to say, only to find that when the time came to say it, I was unable to. The reason for this, I believe, is that in thinking about a topic, we often allow ourselves conceptual gaps that we hardly know exist. When we attempt to communicate our thoughts, however, these gaps become obvious. Organizing and then writing down our thoughts enable us to discover what gaps have yet to be filled.

Misconception #2: *The important thing is what you say, not how you say it.*

As a college student, I was mystified to find that students who wrote well consistently received better grades on their compositions than did students who wrote poorly. Even in my own compositions, I found that the grades I received seemed less to reflect what I had to say than how I said it. At the time, I was unable to decide whether this pattern in grading resulted from the professors' warped value systems, or from their inability to penetrate the facade of written prose. Whereas their criteria for grading papers might be appropriate for an English course, these criteria seemed inappropriate for courses in subjects like psychology.

As a college professor, I have at last discovered the secret of the mysterious grading practices. The discovery came about in two stages, each one part of the initiation rites new college teachers must go through. The first stage occurred when I found myself having a large number of students' papers to read and very little time in which to read them. I was then sincerely grateful to students who wrote well because I could read their papers quickly and understand what they were saying. I did not have the time to puzzle through every cryptic remark in the poorly written papers, however, and I resented the authors' presenting their ideas in a way that did not enable me to understand or evaluate them properly. I also found myself with no desire to reward the authors for this state of affairs. If their ideas were good, they should have taken the time to explain them clearly.

The second stage of discovery occurred when I found myself with just a few seminar papers to read, and plenty of time in which to read them. Now, I thought, I can be fair both to students who write well and to those who do not. I was quickly disabused of this notion. I discovered that whereas it is usually easy to distinguish well-presented good ideas from well-presented bad ideas, it is often impossible to distinguish poorly presented good ideas from poorly presented bad ideas. The problem is that the professor's comprehension of what the student says is solely through the student's way of saying it. Professors can't read minds better than anyone else. If an idea is presented in a sloppy, disorganized fashion, how is one to know whether this reflects the quality of the idea or merely the quality of its presentation?

The question is not easily answered. In one case, I had talked to a student beforehand about what he was going to say, and I expected an outstanding paper on the basis of these conversations. During our conversations, certain details had not been clarified, but I expected these details to be clarified in the paper. Instead, the same ideas that had been inadequately explained in the conversations were inadequately explained in the paper as well. Either the student was unable to clarify these ideas for himself, or he was unable to clarify them for others. The outcome for the reader is the same: confusion and disappointment.

A comparable situation exists for researchers. One quickly notices that the best and most well-known psychologists are also among the best writers. Although there are exceptions, they are infrequent: Poorer writers have fewer readers. One reason for this is that poorly written articles are usually rejected by journal editors. Although journal editors are willing to make minor editorial changes in the articles they receive, they are usually unwilling to publish or rewrite poorly written articles. Even if a poorly written article is accepted and published, however, the psychologist who receives a journal with 5 to 20 articles in it does not want to spend his limited time reading such an article. It is therefore important that you learn now how to present your ideas in a readable fashion.

Misconception #3: *Longer papers are better papers, and more papers are better yet.*

Until my first year of teaching, I believed that longer papers were better papers. Teachers had for years told me and my classmates that they didn't evaluate papers on the basis of length, but I viewed their remarks as a benign ruse designed to discourage length for its own sake. I changed my viewpoint when I started reading students' papers. Evaluating papers on both quality and quantity of ideas, I found little relation between either of these two criteria and the length of students' papers. Sometimes students wrote longer papers because they had more to say; other times they wrote longer papers because it took them several pages to say what could have been said in several sentences. There is nothing wrong with length per se so long as length is not used as a substitute for tight organization and clear writing.

Rather than writing longer papers, some people have taken the alternate route of writing more papers. Why say in one paper what can be said in two for twice the credit? This kind of mentality meets the needs of people who count publications, but not of those who read publications. An integrated series of related experiments will have more impact if published as a single, tightly knit package, than if published as a string of hastily written articles, none of them of much interest in itself.

Misconception #4: *The main purpose of a psychology paper is the presentation of facts, whether newly established (as in reports of experiments) or well established (as in literature reviews).*

A common misconception among the general public is that the goal of science is the accumulation of facts. This misconception is fostered by popular scientific writing that emphasizes scientific findings, which may be easy to describe, at the expense of explanations of these findings, which may be both diverse and difficult to describe. Diverse explanations, however, are the hallmark of science.

Students in introductory psychology courses are prone to this misconception, and it carries over into their writing. I could cite numerous examples of this carry-over, but one in particular comes to mind. I received about a year ago a beautifully written paper reviewing the literature on the testing of infant intelligence. This was one case, however, in which flowing prose was insufficient to obtain a high grade. The paper was flawed in two respects. First, the author made no effort to interrelate the various attempts to measure infant intelligence. Each attempt was described as though it had been made in isolation, even though the various attempts to measure infant intelligence have drawn upon each other. Second, the evaluative part of the paper consisted of a single sentence in which the author stated that it is still too early to draw final conclusions regarding the relative success of the various infant intelligence tests. This sentence is literally true: It is too early to draw *final* conclusions. But it will be too early to draw final conclusions as long as new data about the tests continue to be collected. Since data will continue to be collected for the foreseeable future, and since the tests date back to the early part of the twentieth century, it now seems appropriate to draw at least tentative conclusions. In writing a psychology paper, you must commit yourself to a point of view, even if you may change your mind later on. If the evidence on an issue is scanty, by all means say so. But draw at least tentative conclusions so that the reader knows how you evaluate what evidence is available.

Your paper should be guided by your ideas and your point of view. Facts are presented in service of ideas: to help elucidate, support, or refute these ideas. They provide a test against which the validity of ideas can be measured. You should therefore select the facts that help clarify or test your point of view and omit facts that are irrelevant. In being selective, however, you must not select only those facts that support your position. Scientists demand that scientific reporting be scrupulously honest. Without such honesty, scientific communication would collapse. Cite the relevant facts, therefore, regardless of whose point of view they support.

Misconception #5: *The distinction between scientific writing on the one hand and advertising or propaganda on the other is that the purpose of scientific writing is to* inform *whereas the purpose of advertising or propaganda is to* persuade.

Successful advertising or propaganda need only persuade. Successful scientific writing must both inform and persuade. Students often believe that a successful piece of scientific writing need only inform the reader of the scientist's data and his interpretation of the data. The reader is then left to decide whether the theory provides a plausible account of these (and possibly other) data. This conception of scientific writing is incorrect.

When a scientist writes a paper, he or she has a product to sell. The product is his or her set of ideas about why certain phenomena exist. Occasionally, it is the only product on the market, and he or she need only convince the consumer to buy any product at all. Whether or not the scientist is successful will depend in part upon how persuasive he or she is, and in part upon how much the product is needed. No advertising campaign is likely to sell flowers that are guaranteed not to germinate, nor an explanation of why people don't normally stand on their heads rather than on their feet. In most cases, however, there is an already established demand for the product. Because competing salesmen are trying to corner the market, the scientist must persuade the consumer not just to buy any product, but to buy his or her product.

One of the most common mistakes students make is to sell the wrong product: They misjudge the contribution of their work. I recently received a paper that was full of good, original ideas. The presentation of these ideas, and of other people's as well, was unusually lucid. The only major problem with the paper was that the discussion of the original ideas was condensed into one paragraph buried inconspicuously in the middle of the paper, whereas the discussion of other people's ideas spanned about 10 pages, starting on page 1. The contribution of this paper should have been in its new perspective on an old problem. But the author had de-emphasized this potentially significant contribution in favor of a relatively unimportant one: providing a well-written but unexciting review of other people's perspectives. The hurried reader will usually take the author's emphasis at face value. In this case, the reader might conclude that the paper did not have much of an original contribution to make.

At the opposite extreme, it is possible to dwell so heavily on the contribution of your paper that the contribution is actually muted. I learned this lesson the hard way. A colleague and I wrote a paper intended *(a)* to compare different measures of a psychological construct called subjective organization, and *(b)* to demonstrate that one of these measures is superior to all the rest (Sternberg & Tulving, 1977). We compared the measures on a number of different criteria. One measure proved to be superior to the rest on every one of these criteria. Despite my colleague's warnings, I explicitly called attention to this fact several times in the paper. Leaving nothing to chance, I pointed out the inescapable conclusion that one measure is better than all the rest, and therefore should be the measure of choice.

We submitted the paper for publication, and several months later received two scathing reviews. We were attacked for making what both reviewers believed to be exorbitant claims. According to the reviewers, we had by no means developed an open-and-shut case in favor of the measure we claimed was best. I thought that the arguments made by the reviewers were weak and in some cases plainly incorrect. I was so annoyed with the whole affair that I let the paper sit on my shelf for about a year. Rereading the paper and the reviews a year later, I still believed the reviewers were on the wrong track. My colleague and I decided to tone down our claims for our preferred measure, however, while retaining the same basic line of argument. We resubmitted the paper, and this time received a very favorable review. We achieved much more effective results by understating our case than we had by overstating it, an outcome my colleague (but not I) had anticipated from the start. My subsequent experiences have confirmed repeatedly that in psychology papers, a soft selling technique is more successful than a hard selling technique. By using the latter, you invite a reaction against you as salesman that is likely to hurt the sale of your product. I can recall numerous occasions on which I refused to buy a product because I detested a pushy salesman. In writing the first draft of the paper on measures of subjective organization, I unwittingly occupied the role of the pushy salesman, and I received what should have been a predictable response.

Misconception #6: *A good way to gain acceptance of your theory is by refuting someone else's theory.*

A surprisingly common ploy in scientific papers, even

some published in prestigious journals, is to resort to explanation by default. Whereas students may not know better, professionals should. The investigator describes two (or more) theories of the well-known XYZ phenomenon. He or she then presents devastating evidence against all theories except one. He or she concludes on the basis of this evidence that this one theory is correct.

This indirect method of proof is compelling only when the two (or more) alternatives are *(a)* mutually exclusive and *(b)* exhaustive. Mutually exclusive alternatives are ones in which one outcome precludes the other(s). If a coin lands heads, for example, it cannot at the same time land tails. Exhaustive alternatives are ones that include all possible outcomes. A flip of a coin can result in heads or tails, but nothing else.

The ploy described above has been used in some (but by no means all) research studying sources of differences between groups in intelligence test scores. A study would be presented in which obtained differences in test scores could not be attributable to environmental factors. The author would conclude on this basis that the differences must be due to hereditary factors. These alternatives, however, are neither mutually exclusive nor exhaustive. First, it is possible, indeed, probable, that both heredity and environment influence intelligence test scores. Second, a further source of influence upon intelligence test scores is the interaction between heredity and environment—the effect produced by their joint influence. As an example, certain genes for intelligence may manifest themselves only under favorable environmental conditions.

One other disadvantage of the indirect method of proof bears mention. Criticism of other people's theories often gains one more opponents than it does converts to one's own theory. This was another lesson I learned the hard way. I once wrote a paper that had two major goals: *(a)* to show that my theory of a phenomenon was correct; *(b)* to show that someone else's theory of the phenomenon was incorrect. I presented what I believed was strong evidence in favor of my theory and in opposition to the other person's theory. I submitted the paper to a journal, and it was rejected. The main reviewer of the paper, predictably enough, was the other theorist. It is a common practice to send papers attacking Theory X to Theorist X, with the editor then using his judgment as to whether the review is a fair one. The reviewer criticized not the positive aspect of my paper, but its negative aspect. He argued that our theories actually dealt with somewhat different aspects of the phenomenon under investigation, so that there was no need to attack his theory in the process of supporting my own.

In retrospect, I think the reviewer probably had some valid points; I also think he overreacted. In papers I've reviewed that attack my work, I've probably overreacted as well. Scientists have a reputation among the general public for being objective seekers and impartial evaluators of the truth. I think this reputation is generally deserved, but only when it comes to each other's work. When it comes to their own work, scientists lose their objectivity. When a scientist is attacked, he or she behaves in much the same manner as anyone else under attack. When someone lunges at you with a fist flying toward your face, you don't stop to reflect upon the various considerations that may have led your opponent to attack you. You counterattack. Because scientists are personally so involved in their work, they often treat an attack on their work as a personal attack, even if there is no rational basis for treating it as such. The result can be a personal confrontation in which scientific issues are placed on the back burner.

In conclusion, it is wise to stress the positive contribution of your paper. This does not mean that you should forego criticizing other theories. Such criticism may be essential to your point. If it is, keep in mind my earlier admonition that understatement is a more effective means of persuasion than overstatement. Avoid statements that can be interpreted as contentious but lacking in substance. And if you publish your paper, don't expect the investigator you criticize to congratulate you on your cogent refutation of his work.

Misconception #7: *Negative results that fail to support the researcher's hypothesis are every bit as valuable as positive results that do support the researcher's hypothesis.*

Because science is a fair game, the scientist wins some and he or she loses some. Students often believe that the only honest course of action is for the scientist to report his or her losses as well as his or her wins. To do otherwise would seem to present a false picture of both the scientist and the state of nature.

After reading a diverse sampling of journal articles, the student is bound to arrive at one of two conclusions—either scientists have uncannily sound intuitions about the way experiments will turn out or they maintain closets full of unsuccessful and unreported experiments. Although scientists usually have at least fairly sound intuitions about how experiments will turn out, the state of the journals is more a reflection of well stocked storage closets than of unerring intuitions.

Scientists' failures to report failures are attributable not to their dishonesty, but to the frequent uninterpretability of negative results. Suppose, for example, that an investigator predicts that giving children rewards after learning will increase their learning. The investigator conducts an experiment with two groups. In one group, children receive rewards after learning; in the other group, they do not receive rewards. The investigator finds no difference in learning between groups. What can he or she conclude? Unfortunately, not much. Whereas a significant difference between groups would have provided good evidence that rewards can facilitate learning, absence of a significant difference could be explained in a number of ways, most of them uninteresting. Consider three such uninteresting explanations:

(1) The reward used in the study did not prove a powerful enough incentive. If the reward, for example, was a peanut, then children's cravings for a single peanut might not have been strong enough to increase their efforts to learn.

(2) The sample of children might not have been large enough. It is a well known rule of statistics that if any treatment effect exists at all, then it can be discovered if one's sample is large enough. A small effect may be detectable only with a relatively large sample. If there were only three children in each group, then the investigator might have failed to detect the effect of the reward.

(3) The measure of learning might have been inadequate. Suppose, for example, that the task was to learn the set of multiplication facts for one-digit numbers, and that the measure of learning was a single multiplication fact. This measure probably would have been inadequate to detect learning in either group, and hence a difference in learning between groups.

Under two sets of circumstances, negative results can be of interest:

(1) An investigator repeatedly fails to replicate someone else's results. Suppose someone reports that subjects who stand on their heads for 30 seconds prior to taking a test of visual-motor coordination perform better on the test than control subjects who do not stand on their heads. Another investigator, suspicious of this result, tries to replicate it with two groups of subjects, and fails. Realizing that his or her failure to replicate the result may be due to sampling fluctuations, the investigator tests two more groups of subjects, and again finds no significant difference between groups. At this point, he or she feels ready to report the results. Whereas one failure to replicate a result is not informative, repeated failures to replicate can be informative. The number of failures needed de-

pends in large part upon the strength of prior evidence in support of the result in question. Two failures are probably more than adequate for the "headstand hypothesis," whereas a great many failures would be needed to overthrow a more well-established result such as that under normal circumstances learning increases with practice.

(2) A significant result vanishes when a methodological weakness is corrected. Suppose that the experimenter who wrote the "headstand" paper knew which subjects had stood on their heads, and which had not. This aspect of the methodology suggests a possible bias in the experimenter's scoring of the coordination test (especially if the experimenter is Public Relations Director of the American Association for the Advancement of Acrobatics). A worthwhile methodological refinement would be to conduct the experiment under circumstances in which the experimenter does not know which subjects stood on their heads and which did not. A negative result would be of interest in this case, since it would suggest that the significant difference between groups in the first experiment was due to experimenter bias.

Misconception #8: *The logical development of ideas in a psychology paper reflects the historical development of ideas in the psychologist's head.*

If one were to take journal articles at face value, one would conclude that scientific results come in neat, attractively wrapped packages. One need only go through a uniform series of well-defined steps in order to insure delivery of such packages:

(1) The scientist starts with some clever ideas about a phenomenon, which he explains in the introduction to the paper. These ideas are carefully formulated before the scientist has collected any data, and the data merely serve to confirm (or in rare cases disconfirm) their validity.

(2) The scientist tests these ideas by carefully choosing variables that can be manipulated in a controlled experiment. The scientist's deep understanding of the phenomenon under observation and of scientific method enable him or her to choose the correct variables and experimental manipulation on his or her very first attempt, which he or she describes in the *Method* section of the paper.

(3) The scientist performs the experiment, presenting in the *Results* section of his or her paper the outcomes of data analyses scrupulously planned in advance.

(4) The scientist finally reflects upon the broader implications of the results, presenting his or her reflections in the *Discussion* section of the paper.

I doubt that 1% of the papers published in scientific journals developed in a way even remotely resembling the outline sketched above. Yet, the large majority of published papers are written as though they had developed in this way, or in some way closely resembling it. Let us reconsider the series of steps:

(1) Before carrying out an experiment, one usually has only a vague and tentative idea of what the outcome will be, if only because there are so many possible outcomes that one can scarcely even enumerate them all. One's ideas develop along with the experiment.

(2) One sometimes finds oneself performing the right experimental manipulation on the wrong variables, or the wrong experimental manipulation on the right variables. In order to avoid wasting large amounts of time and money, scientists frequently conduct small-scale pilot experiments that test the feasibility of the experiment as designed. Adjustments in method can then be made in preparation for the full-scale experiment, or the experiment can be scrapped altogether.

(3) Major data analyses are usually planned in advance. Indeed, it is necessary to do this in order to assure that the

design of the experiment permits one to analyze the data in the most advantageous way. Minor data analyses are frequently decided upon after the data have been collected. Often the results of a planned data analysis will suggest a subsequent unplanned one. Only a fool fails to go where the data lead him. One of the most valuable skills a scientist can have is a knack for getting the most out of his or her data. A given set of data can be analyzed in an infinite number of ways, some of them more revealing than others. The scientist must select a small number of ways that are likely to yield maximum payoff.

(4) Ideas for the *Discussion* section of a paper usually start forming at the same time the experiment does, not merely after it has been completed. The reason for this is simple. Unless the experiment has at least some potentially broad and interesting implications, or unless it can lead to some sensible next step in research, it is probably not worth doing.

Why does the picture of research presented by journal articles correspond so poorly to the actual state of affairs? There are at least three reasons:

(1) Journals operate under severe space limitations. A large percentage of articles submitted to the journals must be rejected for lack of space. In some journals, more than 90% of the submitted articles are rejected. Those articles that are accepted must be as concise as possible. An "autobiographical" form of presentation, describing all one's false starts and initial misjudgments, consumes a great deal of space. This space is more profitably devoted to other articles.

(2) An autobiographical account of an experiment tends to be of more interest to oneself than to one's colleagues. An associate recounted to me the way in which he learned this lesson. He submitted a 20-page theoretical article to one of the most prestigious psychological journals. He spent the first 19 pages of the article describing how he had come to his conclusions after a lengthy series of false starts; he presented his final

conclusions on the twentieth page. The article was rejected, not because the final conclusions were still wrong, but because the editor believed that there was only one publishable page in the article—the last. The editor was interested in the psychologist's conclusions, but not in the lengthy soul searching the psychologist had done to arrive at them.

(3) The object of description in a scientific report is a phenomenon and its explanation, not the reporter of the phenomenon and explanation. The focus of the report must reflect this. A graduate student and I recently completed an experiment investigating the development of reasoning skills in children at the second, fourth, and sixth grade levels. Children were presented with reasoning problems, which they were then asked to solve. Since the experiment involved a considerable investment of time and money, we decided to pretest our reasoning problems on some colleagues' children. Our original plan had been to use number of problems correctly solved as the dependent measure. We discovered, however, that even the youngest children made almost no errors on the problems once they fully understood the task. We therefore changed our dependent measure when we did the full-scale experiment, using response time to solve problems correctly instead of number of problems correctly solved. Had someone else planned this experiment, he or she might have realized immediately that the problems were too easy to use number correct as the dependent measure; or he or she might have stumbled longer than we did until the discovery that the problems were too easy. A description of this trial-and-error process is slightly informative about the development of the investigator's intuitions; but it is uninformative about the object of the investigation, in our case, the development of reasoning in children. The scientifically informative statement is that the problems were of a level of difficulty that made response time an appropriate dependent measure.

There is often a fine line between the omission of auto-biographical information and the omission of critical details. If a hypothesis is *post hoc,* then one is obliged to indicate this.

In sum, the steps one follows in planning and carrying out research do not neatly correspond to the successive sections of the psychology paper. In the next two chapters, we will consider the steps in carrying out library and experimental research, and how to describe them in the psychology paper.

CHAPTER 2

Steps in Writing the Library Reseach Paper

Most undergraduate research papers, and many graduate and professional research papers as well, are based upon library research. Library research can proceed smoothly if you follow a sequence of simple steps.

Deciding upon a Topic for a Paper

Your first task is to decide upon a topic for a paper. This is, in a sense, the most important task because the paper can be no better than the topic. I have found five mistakes that repeatedly turn up in students' choices of topics:

THE TOPIC DOESN'T INTEREST THE STUDENT

Many students put off thinking about their choice of topic until the latest possible date. They then find themselves pressed to select a topic, and hastily decide upon something that is of only marginal interest to them. Procrastination in thinking about a topic is a mistake because interesting topics don't often pop into your head overnight. So allow yourself plenty of time to think of a topic. Then, if you are unhappy with the first few ideas that come to mind, you can try out others before you resign yourself to a topic that doesn't interest you. Unless you are at least somewhat interested in the topic you pick, you will find the experience of doing library research a deadly bore, and your paper will probably show it. Having once written and having now read a large number of student papers, I am convinced that a major determinant of quality is the degree of interest the student sustains in the topic about which he or she writes.

THE TOPIC IS TOO EASY OR TOO SAFE FOR THE STUDENT

The purpose of student papers is for the student to learn something about some topic. It is therefore to the student's advantage to select a topic with which he or she is relatively (although not necessarily totally) unfamiliar. Students sometimes seek to optimize safety (or grades) rather than learning, however, choosing a topic with which they are quite familiar. I saw an example of such a choice last year in my Theories of Intelligence course. A student showed in class that she was quite familiar with the literature on creativity in children, perhaps because she had previously written a paper on it. Her remarks in class also showed, however, that she had little background in other areas covered by the course. I was therefore disappointed when she proposed to write a paper on creativity in children. Although she could probably learn something from writing such a paper, it was clear that she had more to gain by selecting a topic from one of the many areas in which she had little background.

THE TOPIC IS TOO DIFFICULT FOR THE STUDENT

The opposite problem from that discussed above is the selection of a topic that is too difficult for the student. In my Theories of Intelligence course I also had a student write a paper on the heritability of intelligence. The student was obviously interested in the topic and wanted to do a good job, but he found that most of the literature went over his head. Understanding the literature on inherited traits requires a knowledge of certain advanced statistical concepts that most undergraduates have not yet encountered. Consequently, it is not possible for them to write a really sophisticated paper on this topic unless they are prepared to learn the necessary statistics. This task is both difficult and time-consuming. In general, you should make certain that the topic you choose does not require understanding of concepts that your background does not permit you to grasp.

THERE IS INADEQUATE LITERATURE ON THE TOPIC

For various reasons, some of the potentially most interesting topics in psychology have been little investigated. In some cases, people simply haven't thought much about the topics; in other cases, they have thought about the topics but found that they did not lend themselves to experimental (or other types of) analysis. These topics are not suitable for literature reviews. Before committing yourself to a topic, make sure that there is adequate literature on it. As a student, I was interested in how people understand proverbs. The topic seemed to deal with a psychologically important function (one that is tested in several intelligence tests), and seemed to have considerable real-world relevance. I found almost no relevant experimental literature, however. Although there was more literature on related topics, such as metaphor, it was obvious that my tentative choice of a paper topic would have to be changed.

THE TOPIC IS TOO BROAD

The most common mistake that students make in the selection of a topic is to select one that is too broad. This problem is understandable, since before writing the paper, students have only a vague idea of how much literature has been published on a given topic. Textbooks usually only scratch the surface, and it is not until one delves into primary sources that one discovers the extent of the relevant literature.

Once you tentatively decide upon a topic, it is a good idea to start compiling a list of references, and to scan some of these references quickly, before starting note-taking in preparation for writing the paper. By following this procedure, you avoid the pitfall of too broad (or too narrow) a topic. By narrowing your topic before you start note-taking, you save yourself the time wasted on taking notes that later will prove of no use in writing the paper.

If you have settled upon a topic that proves to be too broad, you should consider ways in which you can narrow the topic without abandoning it altogether. Consider as an example the topic *Problem Solving*. A search of the available references quickly reveals that this topic is too broad. This topic (and others) might be narrowed in any of several ways:

(1) *Restriction by age.* The review is limited to problem solving in adults or children or infants.

(2) *Restriction by species.* Only problem solving in humans or in rats is considered.

(3) *Restriction by clinical type.* The review deals with problem solving only by normals, or by the mentally retarded, or by the pathological.

(4) *Restriction by psychological perspective.* The review is of the behavioristic, information-processing, or psychometric approach to problem solving; or the review compares these perspectives, dealing only with issues that are relevant to the comparison.

(5) *Restriction by content.* The review deals only with the solution of verbal, or mathematical, or spatial problems.

There are obviously many ways in which you can limit the scope of your topic, and the best way will depend upon the topic, the available literature on the topic, and your interests. Be sure to state in the opening paragraphs of your paper what restrictions you have imposed. A good title will also help the reader understand how you have limited your topic.

Searching the Literature

I have found it useful to maintain two sets of note cards when conducting a literature review. These two sets are author cards and topic cards.

AUTHOR CARDS

Format of author cards. Use small (3″ x 5″) index cards for author cards. You should record on these cards all the information you will later need in order to compile the references for your paper. Each source should be documented. The form of documentation differs somewhat depending upon the nature of the source:

(1) *Journal articles.* Your documentation for journal articles should include *(a)* the author's last name, and first and middle initials, *(b)* the title of the article, *(c)* the name of the journal, *(d)* the year of publication, *(e)* the volume number, and *(f)* the page numbers of the article. An example author card would look like this:

Janis, I. L., & King, B. T. The influence of role-playing on opinion change. *Journal of Abnormal and Social Psychology,* 1954, *49,* 211–218.

(2) *Books.* Your documentation for books should include *(a)* the author's last name, and first and middle initials, *(b)* the title of the book, *(c)* the city in which the book was published, *(d)* the name of the publisher, and *(e)* the year of publication. If the city of publication is not well known, include the state as well. Include the country if the city is not in the United States and is not well known. For example,

Festinger, L. *A theory of cognitive dissonance*. Evanston, Illinois: Row, Peterson, 1957.

In this case, the author does not use a middle initial.

(3) *Edited books.* Your documentation for articles in edited books should include *(a)* the author's last name, and first and middle initials, *(b)* the title of the article, *(c)* the editor of the book, *(d)* the title of the book, *(e)* the city in which the book was published, *(f)* the name of the publisher, *(g)* the year of publication, and *(h)* the pages of the book in which the article appears. For example,

Webb, E. J., & Salancik, J. R. Supplementing the self-report in attitude research. In G. F. Summers (Ed.), *Attitude measurement*. Chicago: Rand McNally, 1970. Pp. 317–327.

Advantages of author cards. Although this system of documentation may appear cumbersome when you do your research, it will have several advantages later on:

(1) *You will have a complete set of references.* There is no possibility of forgetting any sources you need, since you recorded all your sources at the one time when you can't forget them—the time you used them.

(2) *You will have complete documentation for each reference.* Students sometimes keep a complete list of references, but fail to keep complete documentation on each reference. They must then relocate the references later on—if they can find them—to complete the documentation.

(3) *Your References section of the paper will be all but done.* When you are ready to type this section, simply reorder the author cards alphabetically, and type the information from the card.

TOPIC CARDS

Format of topic cards. Large cards (5″ x 7″) are preferred for topic cards. You should record on each card *(a)* the name of the topic at the top, *(b)* information about that topic, *(c)* the source of each item of information, and *(d)* comments.

Only one topic goes on each card. Each time you encounter a new topic on which you want to take notes, make a new topic card. You will save time later on if you avoid multiple topic cards that express the same topic in different ways. For example, the topics *Rorschach Test* and *Inkblots Test* can be combined (unless more than one inkblots test is used).

Your notes on each topic should be complete enough so that you will not have to return to your sources later. Avoid extraneous words that convey no useful information. In taking notes on arguments, make sure you capture the gist of the argument so that later you can reconstruct the author's point of view.

For each statement you compile, record the source by writing down the author's last name and the date of publication. If you make a direct quotation or paraphrase, be sure to indicate this in your notes, citing appropriate page numbers.

When you make comments on a source or the information supplied in it, indicate clearly on the topic card that the comment is yours and not the author's. The best time to make comments on what you read is often when you read it, since at that time the material and its context are freshest in your mind. These comments will be valuable to you later on, since you will be expected in your paper to evaluate information as well as to summarize it. In reading through psychological literature, you should be constantly evaluating five characteristics of the author's arguments:

(1) *Validity of arguments.* On what basis does the

author make each argument? Are the arguments properly substantiated? How? Almost any psychologist who has reviewed papers for a journal (or read student papers) becomes very sensitive to the question of proper validation. A surprisingly common ploy is for an author to present a theory, which may well be plausible, design an experiment or marshall evidence to test some other theory, which also may be plausible, and then conclude that the original theory is correct. In reading an article or book, therefore, assure yourself not only that a test of a theory is a strong test, but also that the test is of the theory it is supposed to test.

(2) *Internal consistency of arguments.* Are the arguments consistent, or do they contradict each other? Are the arguments consistent with the author's general point of view? Whereas in validity you are concerned primarily with the relation between arguments and facts, in internal consistency you are concerned primarily with the relation between arguments and other arguments. Authors are often unaware of internal inconsistencies in their own data. As a result, readers sometimes spot contradictions that authors have lived with for many years, blithely unaware of their existence.

(3) *Presuppositions of arguments.* What does the author presuppose in making each argument; especially, what presuppositions does the author make that he or she does not communicate to the reader, or may not even be aware of? Are the presuppositions realistic? Do the presuppositions strengthen or weaken the impact of the arguments? Consider, for example, the statement: "The Bozo theory of cognitive development is incorrect because it is based upon the assumption that cognitive development is continuous." What presuppositions does this statement make? First, it presupposes that the Bozo theory assumes continuity in cognitive development. Second, it presupposes that a theory making this assumption is incorrect. Third, it presupposes (incorrectly, as it turns out)

that there is such a theory as the Bozo theory of cognitive development.

(4) *Implications of arguments.* What are the implications of each argument; especially, what implications does the author overlook? Do the implications strengthen or weaken the impact of the argument? Are these implications consistent with others reached from other arguments? Consider, for example, the statement: "I violently object to violent objections." What is the obvious implication of the statement?

(5) *Importance of arguments.* Is a particular argument an important one, and therefore one you will want to describe in detail in your paper? Or is it unimportant, and hence not worthy of mention, or worthy of mention only in passing? A common flaw in student papers is to emphasize all arguments equally, regardless of their importance. This flaw inevitably reduces the impact of the paper as a whole.

By keeping in mind these five criteria for evaluating the literature you read, and by writing down your evaluative comments immediately subsequent to the relevant argument, you will supply yourself with much of the substance you will later need to write your paper. Later on, of course, you can always expand upon or change your evaluation. But you will have your evaluative notes from the topic cards to work with, rather than having to start from scratch.

Advantages of topic cards. By compiling your notes on topic cards, several advantages will result:

(1) *When you are ready to write your paper, you will have available to you all the information you need to write it.* You won't have to do any more library work at the last minute when you may no longer have time to do it.

(2) *You will have available to you the source of each argument or piece of information.* You won't have to try to remember who said what.

(3) *You will find it easier to organize your paper than you might have otherwise.* The reason for this is that the topic cards form the input to the next step, preparing an outline.

Preparing an Outline

USE OF TOPIC CARDS

After you have finished note-taking, you are ready to prepare an outline. The topics on the topic cards form the basis of this outline, since they readily can be used as headings and subheadings. Write down all the topics on one or more pieces of paper. Then, cut out strips of paper, one for each topic. Your job now is to rearrange the topics on the strips of paper to form a logical order of presentation. The various topics need not and should not be at the same level of specificity. Some of the topics form major headings, others form minor headings, and others are nested under these minor headings. You may have to add introductory and concluding sections to the outline, as well as any intermediate headings that are needed for smooth transitions. The lowest level of subordination under each heading should represent a single sentence of the final paper.

TYPES OF OUTLINES

Once you have ordered the headings of your outline, you must decide upon one of three ways in which you can complete the outline (Harris & Blake, 1976). We will discuss the three types of outlines with reference to a miniature example in which we compare two personality tests, the Thematic Apperception Test (TAT) and the Minnesota Multiphasic Personality Inventory (MMPI).

The keyword outline. In this kind of outline, you restrict yourself to keywords at each level of description. For example,

   I.   Introduction
  II.   Content
        A. TAT: pictorial
        B. MMPI: verbal
 III.   Administration
        A. TAT: oral
        B. MMPI: written
  IV.   Scoring
        A. TAT: subjective
        B. MMPI: objective
   V.   Conclusion

The topic outline. In this kind of outline, you use phrases and clauses at each level of description. For example,

   I.   Comparison between the TAT and MMPI
  II.   Type of content
        A. TAT: pictures of people in various settings, some realistic and others not
        B. MMPI: statements describing behaviors or beliefs that the examinee marks as true or false as descriptions of himself
 III.   Mode of administration
        A. TAT: pictures sequentially presented by examiner to subject, who supplies a narrative of events leading to, during, and following from the pictured scene
        B. MMPI: booklet containing entire set of statements given to subject, who proceeds through the booklet at his own pace

IV.   Method of scoring
    A. TAT: scored subjectively, often using Murray's taxonomy of needs and press
    B. MMPI: scored objectively by means of a separate key for each diagnostic scale

V.   Differences: content, administration, scoring

The sentence outline.   In this kind of outline, you use complete sentences at each level of description. For example,

I.   This outline compares the TAT and MMPI with respect to content, administration, and scoring.

II.   The tests differ in type of content.
    A. The TAT consists of a series of pictures of people in various settings, some realistic and others not.
    B. The MMPI, on the other hand, consists of a series of statements describing behaviors or beliefs that the examinee marks as either true or false as descriptions of himself.

III.   The tests also differ in mode of administration.
    A. In the TAT, pictures are sequentially presented by the examiner to the subject, who supplies a narrative of events leading to, during, and following from the pictured scene.
    B. In the MMPI, a booklet containing the entire set of statements is given to the subject, who proceeds through the booklet at his own pace.

IV.   Finally, the tests are scored by different methods.
    A. The TAT is scored subjectively, often using Murray's taxonomy of needs and press.
    B. The MMPI is scored objectively by means of a separate key for each diagnostic scale.

V.   In conclusion, the tests differ substantially in content, administration, and scoring.

Choosing a type of outline.   You should use the type of outline that most facilitates your writing. People vary according to which type of outline they find most facilitating. Some people find a keyword outline most helpful because it organizes their thoughts while leaving them maximum flexibility in actually writing the paper; others find a keyword outline too sparse in content to be of much use. Some people like a sentence outline because it essentially writes their paper for them; others find a sentence outline time-consuming to write, and of no greater use in organizing their thoughts than a topical outline. By experimenting with all three types of outlines, you will learn from your own experience which is most suitable for you.

Organization of outlines.   Outlines can be organized in many ways, and many decisions regarding organization are unique to each particular situation. Five principles of organization, however, are common to all outlines and the papers that evolve from them:

(1) *The organization should include a beginning, a middle, and an end, in which you say what you're going to say, say it, and say what you've said.*   When the reader begins a paper, he or she needs some general statements that tell him or her what the paper is about and how it is organized; without this orientation, he or she may become lost almost as soon as he or she starts the paper. When the reader completes the main part of the paper, he or she needs a summary of the main ideas, and whatever final comments you want to supply; without this review, the reader may not realize what you consider to be your main points.

Suppose that the keyword outline presented earlier had consisted only of a "middle":

    I. Content
        A. TAT: pictorial
        B. MMPI: verbal

II. Administration
    A. TAT: oral
    B. MMPI: written

III. Scoring
    A. TAT: subjective
    B. MMPI: objective

The reader of a paper based upon this outline would encounter immediately a comparison between the content of the TAT and the MMPI, without any idea of what the paper intends to accomplish and how it intends to accomplish it. The reader would finish the paper without any idea of what the author believed to be his or her main points, and of what conclusions the author wanted to draw. Although the main body of the paper is well organized, the reader is left with no sense of direction or purpose in the paper.

(2) *Once you decide upon a principle of organization, stick with it.* Beginning writers often change their way of organizing papers midstream, usually without first informing the reader that the change is about to take place. The change confuses the reader. If you must change your organizing principle, be sure to let the reader know. But avoid the change if possible. Consider the plight of the reader faced with a paper based upon the keyword outline at the left. The original keyword outline is reproduced at the right for comparison:

I. Introduction	I. Introduction
II. Content	II. Content
A. TAT: pictorial	A. TAT: pictorial
B. MMPI: verbal	B. MMPI: verbal
III. TAT	III. Administration
A. Administration: oral	A. TAT: oral
B. Scoring: subjective	B. MMPI: written
IV. MMPI	IV. Scoring
A. Administration: written	A. TAT: subjective
B. Scoring: objective	B. MMPI: objective
V. Conclusion	V. Conclusion

Notice that the outline at the left switches its principle of organization, beginning with topic III. Topic II is organized by theme, whereas topics III and IV are organized by test. The outline at the left makes obvious what the careless writer hopes will remain hidden—that the paper is confusing and the author is confused.

(3) *Organize your writing thematically.* Thematic organization enhances the clarity of a paper. The keyword outline as originally presented was organized thematically. The three themes were content, administration, and scoring. The reader would complete a paper based upon this outline with a clear idea of how the TAT and MMPI differ in these three respects. Compare this original outline, presented at the right, to the new outline presented at the left. This new outline is organized by test:

I. Introduction	I. Introduction
II. TAT	II. Content
A. Content: pictorial	A. TAT: pictorial
B. Administration: oral	B. MMPI: verbal
C. Scoring: subjective	III. Administration
III. MMPI	A. TAT: oral
A. Content: verbal	B. MMPI: written
B. Administration: written	IV. Scoring
C. Scoring: objective	A. TAT: subjective
IV. Conclusion	B. MMPI: objective
	V. Conclusion

The organization by test in the outline at the left is not confusing, but it is inferior to the thematic organization at the right. In the thematic organization, the reader can compare the two tests on each theme as he or she reads through the main part of the paper, gradually developing a perspective on how the tests differ. In the organization by test, the reader is unable to begin comparing the tests until he or she is halfway through the main part of the paper. By this time, the reader may have forgotten the characteristics of the first test, since he or she had no motivation to remember them. In reading the section of the paper on the MMPI, he or she probably will have to refer back to the section on the TAT in order to draw a comparison. If the reader is unwilling to spend the time or effort doing what the writer should have done, he or she may never understand the comparison altogether.

The same principle would apply if, say, one wished to compare the viewpoints of Sigmund Freud and Konrad Lorenz on aggression toward oneself, aggression toward others, and aggression toward objects. The preferred way to organize the paper would be by the successive themes of aggression toward self, others, and objects, not by the successive authors, Freud and Lorenz.

There are two exceptions to this principle. The first arises when there are no well developed themes in the literature you plan to review. Each theorist, for example, may deal with a different set of issues. The second exception arises when your focus is genuinely upon the objects of comparison rather than upon the themes along which they are compared. In a book presenting theories of personality, for example, the author's emphasis might be upon the individual perspective of each theorist, rather than upon the themes dealt with in their theories.

(4) *Organize your outline hierarchically*. Beginning writers tend to overuse coordination of ideas and to underuse subordination of ideas. If a paper contains a large number of "main" ideas, the reader will have some diffficulty understanding the ideas and more difficulty remembering them. When you find yourself with a large number of "main" ideas, try to subordinate some of them. You will then communicate the same number of ideas at the same time that you increase the effectiveness with which you communicate them.

Suppose that the keyword outline for the tests had taken this form:

    I. Introduction

   II. TAT content: pictorial

  III. MMPI content: verbal

  IV. TAT administration: oral

   V. MMPI administration: written

  VI. TAT scoring: subjective

 VII. MMPI scoring: objective

VIII. Conclusion

Notice that this outline is much harder to follow than the original keyword outline because all ideas are presented at the same level, with no subordination. The outline therefore is much less effective in comparing the two personality tests.

(5) *Organize for your audience.* In arranging your outline, it is essential that you keep your audience in mind. The level of description for each topic in the outline should be appropriate for the target audience; level of description that is adequate for one audience may be inadequate for another. Consider, for example, the original keyword outline presented earlier. The introductory heading has no subheadings subordinated under it. Since the lowest level of subordination under each heading represents one sentence, this introduction will be just one sentence in length. A brief introduction of this kind may be adequate for a professional seeking a one-paragraph description of salient differences between the TAT and the MMPI, but it probably will be inadequate for a layman unfamiliar with personality tests. Such a person requires more orientation to the topic of the exposition. An expanded introduction is therefore appropriate:

    I. Introduction: personality tests

       A. Purpose

       B. General characteristics

       C. Divergences

          1. Personality tests in general

          2. TAT and MMPI in particular

The general reader will now be able to follow the remainder of the exposition.

Advantages of outlines. Students often wonder whether outlines are worth the time and trouble. Using an outline has three advantages that more than offset the extra work they require:

(1) *Outlines help you organize your writing.* In writing the actual paper, organization will be just one of many concerns you have. Because there are so many different things to keep track of in writing the paper, and because your capacity to keep track of many things at once is limited, organization will receive only limited attention. Since organization of a paper is so important, however, it pays to insert a step prior to writing the paper in which you can devote your full attention to organizing the paper.

(2) *Outlines avert omission of relevant topics.* In doing your research or in compiling your topic cards, you may have inadvertently omitted a topic that you intended to or should have thought to include in your paper. Omissions are much easier for the author to spot in an outline than in a paper. They are also much easier to correct before writing of the paper has begun.

(3) *Outlines avert inclusion of irrelevant topics.* Authors sometimes find that a topic that had seemed relevant to the paper in the early stages of research no longer seems relevant when the research is being organized. Irrelevant material shows itself in an obvious way during preparation of an outline, since the material seems to have no place in the outline. By discovering irrelevancies during preparation of the outline, the author can discard them so that later they do not distract him or her in writing the paper.

Writing the Paper

This section of the chapter is briefer than the previous ones because most of the principles that apply to writing library research papers apply to experimental papers as well, and these principles are discussed in later chapters. In writing the library research paper you should keep in mind particularly the five criteria for evaluating authors' arguments that were described earlier. Readers of your paper will evaluate your paper by the same (or similar) criteria to those you used to evaluate the papers and books you read:

(1) *Validity.* Are your arguments consistent with the literature you reviewed? Have you explained inconsistencies? Have you properly substantiated each of your arguments?

(2) *Internal consistency.* Are your arguments consistent with each other? Are they consistent with your general point of view?

(3) *Presuppositions.* Have you made clear to the reader what you presuppose? Are your presuppositions reasonable ones that the reader is likely to accept? Has the impact of your presuppositions upon your conclusions been discussed?

(4) *Implications.* Have you discussed the implications of your arguments? Are these implications realistic? Do these implications strengthen or weaken your arguments?

(5) *Importance.* Have you emphasized your important arguments and conclusions, and subordinated the less important ones? Have you explained why you view certain arguments and conclusions as important, and others as less so?

By using these five criteria to evaluate your literature review, you will improve its quality. Later, we will consider in more detail criteria for evaluating the quality of all psychology papers.

CHAPTER 3

Steps in Writing the Experimental Research Paper

When a research psychologist talks about "writing a paper," he or she is talking about a lengthy and complicated chain of events that includes a great deal more than just reporting of research results. In this chapter I shall outline these events from start to finish.

Planning Experimental Research

GETTING AN IDEA

For most psychology students, getting an idea for an experiment is the hardest part of research. There are no steps one can take that will guarantee one's coming up with a good idea. The following suggestions may prove helpful, however.

Whom To Consult. In many colleges and universities, the faculty is among the most underutilized of resources. In my first semester of teaching at Yale, I set aside three hours each week for "office hours." I encouraged—sometimes I practically begged—students to come see me during these hours for advice on papers, projects, and the like. I left my door wide open to encourage students to enter. For the most part, though, I sat staring at the walls, or at the people scurrying by (but not in) the door. I also encouraged students to make individual appointments if they were unable to see me during my prearranged hours, but for the most part, students also failed to take me up on this request. More recently, business has picked up, although much more so among graduate than among undergraduate students.

I and many of my colleagues are perplexed by the timidity of students in seeking faculty advice. Recently, the psychology department faculty at Yale spent the better part of an hour trying to figure out why students are so timid in approaching faculty. Sometimes students try once, are unsuccessful in reaching the faculty member, and give up. Sometimes they don't try at all. Faculty members (as well as postdoctoral students and graduate students) can be a student's most helpful first avenue of approach in writing a paper. Students should be more assertive in seeking their advice.

What To Read. Ideas often come out of one's reading. Some kinds of reading are more likely to lead to good ideas than others.

(1) *Pursue a small number of topics in depth.* Most undergraduate psychology courses, and many graduate ones, are not well suited to the stimulation of creative ideas for experiments. This is because they cover a large amount of material superficially, rather than a small amount in depth. In order to come up with a good idea for an experiment, it helps to have a deep understanding of the issues involved in some relatively small area of psychological research. The superficial understanding acquired in survey courses is usually inadequate. Find some topic in or related to your course work that interests you. Then use your course lectures and reading material as guides to the published literature. Pursue the references that your teacher and textbook cite, and pursue the references most frequently cited in these references. By digging into the literature on a topic, you will acquire a deeper

understanding of the issues that are the focus of psychological research.

(2) *Acquaint yourself with research at the frontiers of knowledge.* As an undergraduate, I once followed the advice of the preceding paragraph, only to find myself acquiring a deep understanding of an issue that had ceased to interest psychologists twenty years before. In pursuing a topic, consider whether it is of current interest. Because of the long time lag between the writing and publication of a book, most textbooks are somewhat out of date by the time they are published. Within five to ten years, they usually become hopelessly out of date. As a result, students relying on these textbooks may find themselves generating ideas that someone else thought of several years before. In order to become acquainted with literature on the frontiers of knowledge, scan recent journal articles and make use of the references described in Chaper 7 of this book. Ask your professor or advanced graduate students for leads to the most recently published work on particular topics.

(3) *Start with general readings and proceed to more specific ones.* Because of space limitations, authors of journal articles are often unable to present in detail the previous research that motivated their particular experiments. If you are unacquainted with this previous research, you may find yourself unable to understand the rationale of the experiments. It is therefore wise to start your reading with a review of the relevant literature, if you can find one, or with a theoretical article that compares the major theoretical positions. Reports of individual experiments will make more sense to you if you are first acquainted with the research context in which they were done.

How To Read. How you read is as important as what you read. Suppose, for example, that you read an article testing the theory that repeated exposure to persuasive communications results in attitude change toward the viewpoint advocated by those communications, regardless of one's initial attitudes. You might pursue further research taking you in any one of four directions:

(1) *Extend the theory.* After reading the article, you may be persuaded that the theory is sound and could be extended. You might want to show that repeated exposure to communications advocating a viewpoint, but in a nonpersuasive manner, also results in attitude change toward the position taken by the communications.

(2) *Generate an analogous theory.* If you find the theory and data compelling, you may want to think up an analogous theory. Perhaps repeated exposure to a particular kind of music increases liking for that music. Or perhaps repeated exposure to any kind of communication increases positive affect toward that kind of communication.

(3) *Limit the theory.* Perhaps you believe that the conclusion derived from the data is too broad. If the subjects in the experiment were all children, for example, you may wish to show that the theory is applicable only to children. Or if the communications used in the experiment were all health-related ones, you may want to show that the theory is applicable only to arguments related to bodily care.

(4) *Challenge the evidence testing the theory.* In reading the article, you may spot a methodological, statistical, or logical flaw in the author's argument. In this case, you may want to test the theory in a way that corrects the flaw. For example, suppose that the author of the paper tested his or her hypothesis merely by showing that after two hours of listening to a set of three persuasive communications, most subjects agreed with the viewpoint advocated by those communications. If the author has not shown, however, that at least some

of his or her subjects disagreed with the viewpoints of the communications prior to the test, then the conclusion does not follow from his or her data.

Drawing upon personal experience. Your own experience can be a valuable source of ideas. You may have found, for example, that you are more likely to conform to group norms if you are only marginally accepted by a peer group than if you are fully accepted by it. Or you may have found that you remember more material if you form vivid images of the words to be remembered than if you merely try to remember the words. Hypotheses such as these should be followed up by a literature review investigating what research has already been done. Even if your particular idea has been investigated, you may then think of another, related idea that has not yet been tested.

SELECTING INDEPENDENT VARIABLES

After you have come up with an idea, you need a way to test it. In order to test the idea, you need one or more independent variables. Independent variables are those variables that are manipulated by the experimenter. In the persuasibility experiment described above, possible independent variables include *(a)* amount of exposure to persuasive communications, *(b)* content of persuasive communications, and *(c)* level of agreement between subjects' initial attitudes and the position advocated by the persuasive communications. Once you have chosen your independent variable(s), you must decide how many and what levels of the independent variable(s) to use. For example, you might include in a persuasibility experiment *(a)* three levels of exposure to the persuasive communications—no exposure, ten minutes of exposure, and one hour of exposure—and *(b)* two communications—one message dealing with capital punishment and one message dealing with compulsory use of seat belts in cars.

In most experiments, there are a large number of potentially interesting independent variables, but it is possible to choose only a small fraction of these. In most experimental designs, each time you add an independent variable to your experiment, you increase the size of your experiment multiplicatively. You must therefore choose your independent variables with care. In the persuasibility experiment, the type font in which the persuasive communications are presented is not likely to affect the outcome of the experiment, and hence would be a poor choice of an independent variable. The medium of communication, oral or written, might affect the outcome of the experiment, and hence would be a possible choice. The amount of exposure to the persuasive communications is almost certain to affect the outcome of the experiment, and hence is a necessary choice.

In selecting independent variables, there is usually a tradeoff between experimental control and ecological validity. Experimental control refers to the ease with which the experimenter can manipulate and later monitor the effects of the independent variables. Ecological validity refers to the generalizability of the obtained results to real-world situations. Total loss of experimental control can lead to uninterpretable results. Disregard of ecological validity can lead to trivial results. Researchers differ widely in the importance they assign to each of these items: Everyone must strike some sort of balance between the two.

SELECTING DEPENDENT VARIABLES

In addition to choosing one or more independent variables, you must select one or more dependent variables. The dependent variable is the variable affected by (dependent upon) the independent variables. It serves as the outcome to be measured. Whereas it is common to choose more than one independent variable in a single experiment, it is relatively uncommon to choose more than one dependent variable. When multiple dependent variables are used, they are usually studied separately, without much attempt to interrelate the outcomes. The major reason for psychologists' reluctance to deal with multiple outcomes is the greater difficulty involved in statistical analysis, not the inability of multiple outcomes to provide more meaningful data than single outcomes.

In most experiments, there are at least several possible dependent variables of interest to choose from, so the choice must be made carefully. In the persuasibility experiment, two possible dependent variables are (a) response to an opinion questionnaire administered at the end of the experimental session, and (b) willingness one month later to join a citizens' lobbying group devoted to the cause advocated by the communication. Note that the first dependent variable measures immediate overt opinion change within the context of the experiment, whereas the latter dependent variable measures delayed covert opinion change outside the context of the experiment. Ideally, an experiment will include both kinds of measures. If only one is to be chosen, the experimenter must evaluate an important tradeoff that frequently confronts psychological researchers. The first measured outcome is much more likely than the second to be influenced by the experimental manipulation, but it is also of much less practical importance. Even if the opinion questionnaire administered at the end of the experiment shows a significant effect of the experimental treatment, one has no assurance that the effect will last for any long period of time, or even for any time beyond the conclusion of the experimental session. The second measured outcome is of considerable practical interest, but in relying upon it, the experimenter may be throwing away any chance of an observable experimental effect. The experimenter must therefore decide upon a dependent variable that gives a reasonable chance of obtaining an outcome that is both statistically and practically significant.

DECIDING UPON BETWEEN—SUBJECTS AND WITHIN—SUBJECTS VARIABLES

Each independent variable can be studied either between subjects or within subjects. A between-subjects independent variable is one in which a given subject receives only one level of the experimental treatment. A within-subjects independent variable is one in which a given subject receives all levels of the experimental treatment.

Return again to the persuasibility experiment. If both independent variables were between-subjects, then each subject would receive (a) either no exposure, ten minutes of exposure, or one hour of exposure to (b) either the communication on capital punishment or that on compulsory use of seat belts. Since there are three levels of the first independent variable and two levels of the second, there are 3 x 2 levels in all, or 6 different experimental groups, each composed of different subjects. If both independent variables were within-subjects, each subject would receive both persuasive communications, and would be tested before receiving the communications, ten minutes after receiving the communications, and one hour after receiving the communications for his current opinion on each.

In some cases, it is easy to decide whether to test a particular variable between subjects or within subjects. In other cases, however, the decision is a difficult one for the experimenter to make, and a potentially consequential one. The experimenter must evaluate a delicate tradeoff. On the one hand, earlier within-subjects treatments may spoil the subject for later treatments. In other words, the subject's receiving one experimental treatment may have unforeseen consequences for his or her responses to subsequent treatments. On the other hand, within-subjects designs guarantee matching of subjects across treatment conditions, because the subjects are the same. This matching can be particularly important when there are relatively small numbers of subjects.

Consider again the design of the persuasibility experiment. Suppose we administer the three opinion questionnaires—before treatment, ten minutes after treatment, one hour after treatment—to the same subjects. We run the risk that the mere answering of an earlier questionnaire will influence subjects' responses to later questionnaires. This influence can contaminate the results and render equivocal any interpretation of them. Suppose that instead we administer the three opinion questionnaires to three different groups of subjects. We then have no way of knowing that our groups are matched in important ways. They may differ in initial level of agreement with the persuasive communication; or they may differ in persuasibility (so that some are more susceptible by nature than others to persuasion attempts); or they may differ in the speed at which they assimilate new information, and hence in the speed at which their attitudes are affected by new information. The list can go on *ad infinitem*. Although random sampling of subjects provides some protection against poor matching of groups, the adequacy of this protection depends upon the size of the sample. Unless groups are quite large, protection may be inadequate. With six different groups in the full design of the persuasibility experiment, it is unlikely that very large groups can be obtained in a reasonably economical way.

A compromise can be worked out whereby all subjects receive the opinion survey before treatment, but only some receive it after ten minutes of treatment, whereas others receive it after one hour. This compromise, however, does not solve the basic dilemma, since the subjects' receipt of the pretest can still affect their performance on the subsequent test. In deciding whether to test a particular variable between subjects or within subjects, the experimenter must decide which kind of risk he or she is more willing to take.

DECIDING HOW DATA WILL BE ANALYZED

Major decisions about data analysis should be made prior to the collection of data. There are two reasons why these decisions should be made in advance. First, statistical tests must be interpreted more cautiously if decided upon *post hoc*. As it is sometimes said, everyone has 20/20 hindsight. Second, if major decisions about data analysis are not made in advance, the experimenter runs the risk of finding later that the experimental design does not permit him or her to analyze the data the way he or she wants to, or to analyze the data at all. Decisions about specific kinds of data analysis require statistical background that is beyond the scope of this book.

SELECTING SUBJECTS

Three major decisions must be made in selection of subjects. First, from what population will subjects be selected? Second, how will subjects be selected from this population? Third, how many subjects will be selected?

The population from which subjects are selected is the population to which the experimental results will be generalizable. Hence, if one is interested in making generalizations to the general population of the United States, then one must select a sample that is representative of the general population of the United States. If one is interested in a population of gifted children, then one must select a sample representative of gifted children. The question of generalizability of results is often quietly placed in the background of an experimental report, if it is discussed at all, because most experiments are conducted on samples that are not representative of the population of interest. Many of the experiments conducted today use college students as subjects, although the experimenters' intent is to generalize the results to the population of adult Americans (or even to adults all over the world).

One faces a tradeoff in deciding upon a population from which to draw subjects. On the one hand, the researcher usually wants to generalize his or her results to as broad a population as possible. On the other hand, subjects are much easier to obtain from some populations than from others. College and university students are often readily available, whereas other groups of adults are much harder to corral into the laboratory.

Subjects can be selected in any of a number of ways from the population. The two most common models of selection are the random and the stratified sample. In a random sampling procedure, the experimenter selects individuals from the population at random. In a stratified sampling procedure, the experimenter selects individuals in a way that assures that major subdivisions of the population are represented in some proportion, usually the population proportion. In practice, it is almost never possible to obtain a purely random or stratified sample, because the entire population is not available to the experimenter. The subjects who are available usually form a biased sample of the population from which they are drawn. Even if one's population is college students, for example, the sample of college students at any one university is inevitably going to be biased.

Decisions about numbers of subjects are usually made on the basis of two considerations. First, how many subjects can be tested feasibly, given the constraints of time, money, and subject availability? Second, how many subjects are needed to show statistical significance for an effect of a certain magnitude? This latter consideration involves statistical concepts beyond the scope of this book. The basic idea, though, is that in order for a small treatment effect to be statistically significant, a large sample is needed. The greater the magnitude of the treatment effect, the smaller the sample size needed to show statistical significance.

CHOOSING EXPERIMENTAL MATERIALS

Four considerations must be taken into account in choosing materials for an experiment:

(1) Do the materials represent a reasonable sample of the universe of materials to which one wants to generalize?

(2) Are there enough materials to obtain generalizable measurements?

(3) Are the materials suitable for the subjects to whom they will be administered?

(4) Are the materials suitable for testing the hypothesis?

Students and psychologists alike tend to pay too little attention to the generalizability of experimental materials. General conclusions about a broad universe of materials are often drawn on the basis of an experiment or several experiments using just one kind of material. Suppose, for example, that an investigator is interested in how people solve syllogisms. A subject is presented with two premises, called the major premise and the minor premise, and a conclusion. The subject's task is to say whether the conclusion follows logically from the premises. A simple syllogism would take the form

(1)	All B are C.	(Major Premise)
	<u>All A are B.</u>	(Minor Premise)
	All A are C.	(Conclusion)

As an investigator, you might vary structural properties of the syllogism. For example, you might substitute for the major premise statements like *Some B are C, No B are C,* and *Some B are not C.*

Your theory of how people solve syllogisms, however, could not be complete unless you took into account content as well as structure. Suppose, for example, that we leave the structure of the syllogism unchanged, varying only its content. Compare the difficulty of the following two syllogisms to each other and to the syllogism above:

(2)   All birds are animals.
          All canaries are birds.
          All canaries are animals.

(3)   All birds are canaries.
          All animals are birds.
          All animals are canaries.

You will probably find, as others have found before you, that the content of the syllogism greatly affects its difficulty. Most people find syllogisms like *(2)* easier to comprehend than syllogisms like *(3)* because the premises of the former syllogism conform to real-world experience, whereas the premises of the latter syllogism violate it. A complete theory of syllogistic reasoning would have to take into account these effects of content, something no theory yet does. The general point, of course, is that no theory can be accepted with confidence unless it has been shown to explain data for a wide variety of experimental materials.

It is important not only to have a relatively broad sampling of materials, but a relatively large sampling as well. The syllogism experiment would be unimpressive if it had three different kinds of content, but only one syllogism of each kind. In order to obtain reliable measurements, it is usually necessary to have at least several replications of each kind of item.

The investigator must take care that his or her experimental materials are suitable for the target subject population. Syllogisms such as the ones above would be suitable for an adult subject population, but not for a population of first-grade children. If these children failed to solve syllogisms like the ones above, the investigator would be unable to determine whether the failure was due to inability to reason syllogistically or due to inability to comprehend the materials. The investigator might use concrete play materials instead of verbal ones. For example, he or she might show the children plastic replicas of animals, and then demonstrate to them that all the elephants are gray, and all the animals with trunks are elephants. The children would then have to indicate whether all the animals with trunks are gray. Special care would have to be taken to ensure that the children understood the nature of the task.

The materials one uses must be appropriate to the hypothesis under investigation. Suppose, for example, that an investigator wants to test the hypothesis that syllogisms with counterfactual conclusions are more difficult to solve than syllogisms with factual conclusions. The following two sets of syllogisms would provide poor tests of this hypothesis:

FACTUAL
CONCLUSIONS

COUNTERFACTUAL
CONCLUSIONS

(1) All integers are rational.
All natural numbers are integers.
_____
All natural numbers are integers.

(1) All rational numbers are natural numbers.
All integers are rational numbers.
_____
All integers are natural numbers.

(2) All sunny days are enjoyable days.
All bright days are sunny days.
_____
All bright days are enjoyable days.

(2) All sunny days are unenjoyable days.
All cloudy days are sunny days.
_____
All cloudy days are unenjoyable days.

The first syllogism is inappropriate because most subjects (except, perhaps, in a population of mathematicians) would not realize which syllogism has a factual conclusion and which has a counterfactual conclusion. The second syllogism is inappropriate because the conclusions (as well as the premises) are matters of opinion; although some people might agree with the first conclusion and disagree with the second conclusion, these agreements and disagreements are not matters of fact.

CHOOSING A MEANS OF PRESENTING EXPERIMENTAL MATERIALS

Experimental materials usually can be presented in many forms. The form of presentation generally is determined largely by convenience, since little is known about the effects of form of presentation upon performance. Investigators usually assume the effects of form of presentation upon performance will be trivial. Suppose, for example, that an investigator is interested in the effect of concreteness upon free recall of a list of words. His or her hypothesis is that more concrete words, like *banana,* will be better recalled than more abstract words, like *freedom.* In order to test this hypothesis, the investigator compares recall of two lists of words, one concrete and the other abstract.

The list of words might be presented either visually or auditorily. If the words are presented visually, they might be presented via flash cards, slides, or possibly a computer terminal. If the words are presented auditorily, they might be presented via word of mouth or tape recorder. Modality of presentation (visual or auditory) and vehicle of presentation (e.g., slides or tape recorder) within modality might affect level of recall, but it is assumed that this effect will be constant across treatment conditions. Thus, if on the average two fewer concrete words are recalled when auditory rather than visual presentation is used, it is assumed that on the average two fewer abstract words will be recalled as well. The investigator is not likely to use both auditory and visual presentation in order to show generality of the hypothesis to both modalities. In some experiments—for example, experiments on vision or audition—modality of presentation will be a critical variable. In most experiments, however, it is considered relatively unimportant. Investigators turn their attention to variables more likely to influence their results.

WRITING DIRECTIONS

Once you have decided upon the experimental task and materials, you have to write directions telling subjects what is expected of them. It is essential that the directions be clear and complete, since unclear or incomplete instructions can result in subjects' doing a task different from that you intend. The directions may be presented auditorily or visually. I usually have the experimenter present the directions aloud while the subject reads them silently. Subjects thereby are exposed to the directions in two modalities.

In the free-recall experiment, the following directions might be used:

Directions for Free-Recall Task

In this task, the experimenter will read aloud a list of words. You should listen carefully to these words. After the experimenter has completed reading the list, he will pause, and then say the word *Recall*. At this point, you should recall as many words as you can from the list in any order you wish. Write your answers on the sheet in front of you. If you are not sure of an item–guess. Your recall will be scored for the number of words correctly recalled.

If you have any questions, please ask them now.

DECIDING UPON A MEANS OF SCORING DATA

Since scoring can be time-consuming, the layout of subjects' response sheets or booklets should be planned carefully in advance. An easy-to-score layout can save many hours of work later on. If the subjects' responses are simple—letters, numbers, words—their answers usually can be recorded in successive columns of each page. An easily readable format such as this one will facilitate scoring, possibly enabling you to devise a stencil key that can be placed either next to or over each column. Stencil keys are frequently used in scoring objective tests, and can be used to equal advantage in scoring of experimental data.

If the data will be keypunched for subsequent computer analysis, it is wise to show your answer sheet layout to a keypuncher before you use it. If the layout is easily readable, the keypuncher (who may be you) may be able to punch the data directly from the answer sheets, bypassing the time-consuming step of coding the data.

WRITING A CONSENT FORM

Several years ago, the United States Department of Health, Education and Welfare (HEW) started requiring experimenters supported by HEW funds to have all subjects sign statements of informed consent prior to participation in experiments. In the case of children, parents were required to sign. More recently, the National Science Foundation (NSF) has also started requiring this step for the protection of human subjects. Experimenters are also required to have their experiments approved by a human subjects committee of their college or university prior to conducting the experiments. In view of the widespread concern today with the protection of subjects, it is probably wise to use consent forms even for informal class projects. A sample consent form (in this case, for an experiment on decision making in groups) is shown on page 56.

The consent form must be modified to meet the needs of each particular experiment. The form must always include,

Declaration of Informed Consent

I give my informed consent to participate in this study of how people make decisions in groups. I consent to publication of study results so long as the information is anonymous and disguised so that no identification can be made. I further understand that although a record will be kept of my having participated in the experiment, all experimental data collected from my participation will be identified by number only.

(1) I have been informed that my participation in this experiment will involve my joining a group faced with a decision to make.

(2) I have been informed that the general purpose of this experiment is to study processes used by groups in making different kinds of decisions.

(3) I have been informed that there are no known expected discomforts or risks involved in my participation in this experiment. This judgment is based upon a relatively large body of research with people solving problems of a similar nature.

(4) I have been informed that there are no "disguised" procedures in this experiment. All procedures can be taken at face value.

(5) I have been informed that the investigator will gladly answer any questions regarding the procedures of this study when the experimental session is completed.

(6) I have been informed that I am free to withdraw from the experiment at any time without penalty of any kind.

Concerns about any aspects of this study may be referred to the Chairman, Committee on the Protection of Human Subjects, Imaginary University, Room 107, Memorial Hall.

_____   _____
(Experimenter)   (Experimental Participant)

                                 _____
                                            (Date)

however, *(a)* a statement of informed consent, *(b)* sufficient information about the experiment so that the subject's consent is truly informed, and *(c)* the subject's signature and the date.

The general purpose of the experiment is explained in item 1. I prefer to leave this explanation vague. First, a detailed explanation might affect the experimental outcome. If, for example, subjects were told that the experiment was designed to investigate interpersonal relations among group members, the subjects might be more cautious in the ways they related to other group members. Second, since subjects are given a detailed debriefing at the end of the experiment, a lengthy description of the experiment at the beginning is redundant.

Subjects must be warned if there are any known expected discomforts. In an experiment requiring a subject to wear lenses that distort his vision, for example, the subject may experience brief discomfort after the lenses are removed. If you have no experience on the basis of which to draw a conclusion, or very little experience, then you are obliged to say so.

I include item 4 because *(a)* subjects are sometimes uneasy about participating in psychology experiments, expecting to be tricked, and *(b)* I never use disguised procedures. If you sometimes use disguised procedures and sometimes do not, however, you may be reluctant to use such an item, since its absence might be interpreted as implying the existence of disguised procedures.

Emphasis upon the technical details of obtaining informed consent can obscure the reason for obtaining it. The important question the experimenter must face is whether his or her experiment places the subject at risk. If so, then the experimenter must examine the risk/benefit ratio: Do the benefits of the research outweigh its risks? Students should consult faculty advisers for additional perspectives on whether subjects' rights are being protected, in particular, their rights to personal privacy and confidentiality. Often, the research will have to be reviewed further by a departmental or university committee in order to assure that subjects receive adequate personal protection.

WRITING A DEBRIEFING SHEET

After the experiment is over, subjects often want to know the purpose of the experiment and the various experimental procedures. Experimenters have a moral obligation, and in some universities, a legal obligation, to debrief subjects about the experiment. The debriefing should be informative and nontechnical. It should inform the subjects of what the experiment is supposed to test, how the experiment tests it, and what the anticipated outcomes are. Debriefing may be oral or written, although I prefer written debriefing since subjects as well as experimenters then have a record of having participated in the experiment. The following is a sample debriefing, in this case for the experiment on decision making in groups.

Experimental Debriefing
Decision Making in Groups

The purpose of this experiment was to further our understanding of decision making in groups. The hypothesis tested by the experiment was that groups will make faster decisions if they are explicitly warned in advance that interpersonal frictions, rivalries, and animosities can impede the group decision-making process, and that therefore group members should take special care not to let these impediments hinder them at the decision-making task.

Four groups participated in the experiment. In two groups, subjects were asked to decide whether the United States should sell nuclear material for "peaceful purposes" to countries that have the capacity to manufacture atomic bombs. In two other groups, subjects were asked to decide in a rational way which two group members would receive a $2 bonus at the end of the experiment. They were informed that the other members would receive no bonus, and that the decision could not be made using a random selection procedure (such as drawing lots). In one "nuclear material" group and in one "$2 bonus" group, subjects were warned in advance not to let interpersonal frictions, rivalries, and animosities impede their decision-making process. The other two groups received no warning of any kind.

It is expected that the forewarned groups will reach a decision faster than the unwarned groups, regardless of whether they are making a decision about "nuclear material" or about the "$2 bonus." The purpose of using two different kinds of decisions was to show the generality of the instructional effect. The experiment is also being repeated four times with different groups of subjects in order to show that the instructional effect is a reliable one. The four repetitions of the experiment will be combined for data analysis.

If you have any questions, please feel free to ask them of the experimenter. If you would like a summary of the results when the research is completed, please leave your name and address with the experimenter.

Thank you for participating.

_____
(Experimenter)

Before debriefing your subjects, it is wise to have your subjects debrief you. After the experiment is over, you should ask your subjects to tell you (preferably in writing) how they went about doing the experimental task. Subjects' comments can provide you with insights that you otherwise would not have obtained.

TESTING PILOT SUBJECTS

Before starting final data collection, you should consider testing pilot subjects. Pilot testing enables you to spot flaws in the experiment before you actually conduct it. You may find that your directions are unclear, that you have not allowed enough time for your subjects to complete the task, or that the task is too difficult for your subjects. The list of possible flaws is endless. Pilot testing is like an insurance policy. By making a small investment in advance, you can save yourself potentially enormous costs later on. The more careful the pilot testing (the larger the insurance premium), the less likely you are to end up with disastrous results (the greater the insurance coverage). I have found that there is almost always some potential problem that is uncovered during pilot testing.

Executing Experimental Research

If you have planned your experiment carefully, execution of the experiment should be straightforward. You should make sure, as much as possible, that extraneous variables are kept constant from session to session. Thus, things like lighting, ventilation, and seating arrangement should not be varied. Outside noise should be minimized. If the experiment involves a number of separate parts, you may want to keep a list so that you do not forget any of them. Experimenters, like subjects, sometimes get distracted; and once data are lost, they are difficult or impossible to replace.

Use the experimental sessions as an informal opportunity to gain insights into how subjects perform the experimental tasks. Subjects occasionally make comments about what they are doing or how they are doing it. Also be on the lookout for nonroutine problems—a subject who stayed up the night before writing a paper and can barely keep his eyes open, a subject who is not paying attention to the experimental task, a flickering lightbulb, an erratic stopwatch. You should write down notes on any unusual problems, and try to correct them. The subject who stayed up all night should be rescheduled; the subject who is not paying attention should be told politely to pay attention; the lightbulb should be replaced; the stopwatch should be fixed or replaced. You will collect much better data if you are aware of problems and correct them immediately.

In theory, the experimenter should be blind to assignment

of subjects to treatments, so that his prior expectations about treatment effects will be unable to influence the experimental results. In practice, the experimenter often knows which subjects have been assigned to which treatments. In reading the word lists for the free-recall experiment, for example, the experimenter will probably recognize whether the words are abstract or concrete. If the experimenter observes the groups in the decision-making experiment, he or she will know whether or not he or she has previously warned them about impediments to group decision making. A voluminous literature exists on experimenter effects upon research results, and there is no question that the experimenter can influence the outcome in subtle ways. The experimenter might read the list of abstract words just a little more quickly or less clearly than the list of concrete words, or he or she might differentially reinforce the decision-making groups with facial expressions. You have a responsibility as experimenter to give your hypotheses the fairest possible test. Subtle and not so subtle experimenter effects undermine the interpretability and credibility of your results. It is therefore essential that you take care not to influence the outcome of your experiment through incidental and (presumably) unintended actions.

Analyzing Data from Experimental Research

After the experiment is completed, you are ready to analyze your data. Techniques for analyzing data are beyond the scope of this book. Two unusually lucid textbooks covering elementary statistical techniques are Minium (1970) and Runyon and Haber (1976). Hays (1973) is more advanced, presenting much of the theory underlying the statistical techniques. A standard reference for analysis-of-variance designs is Winer (1971), and some of these designs are also presented in Hays's book. For description and explanation of multi-variate statistical techniques. I recommend Cooley and Lohnes (1971), Tatsuoka (1971), or Morrison (1976). The books named in this section are listed in order of difficulty. Only the first two books and possibly the third are suitable for most undergraduates. The last three books are suitable only for advanced graduate students.

Reporting Experimental Research

Once you have analyzed your data and thought about your results, you are ready to report them. I suggest that you write an outline prior to writing the paper, just as you would if you were writing a library research paper. A standard format for the outline looks like this:

      Title
      Author's Name and Byline
      Abstract
  I. Introduction
 II. Method
      A. Materials
      B. Apparatus
      C. Subjects
      D. Design
      E. Procedure
III. Results
IV. Discussion
      Reference Notes
      References
      Appendix

TITLE

The title should inform the reader simply and concisely what the paper is about. It is important that the title be self-explanatory. Readers will come across the title in other papers that refer to your paper and in *Psychological Abstracts,* and they may have to decide on the basis of the title alone whether they want to read your paper. The title should include keywords, e.g., the theoretical issue to which the paper is addressed, the dependent variable(s), the independent variable(s). Keywords are important because the title will be stored in information-retrieval networks that rely on such words to determine the relevance of your study to someone else's research interests. For the same reason, it is important to avoid irrelevant and misleading words, since such words may spuriously lead an investigator uninterested in your topic to your paper. The title should not exceed 12 to 15 words in length.

AUTHOR'S NAME AND INSTITUTIONAL AFFILIATION

Write your name as you wish it to be recognized professionally. Thus, you might choose John Jones, John J. Jones, John James Jones, J. Jones, J.J. Jones, or J. John Jones. A first name, middle initial, and last name is the most commonly used form of presentation. Omit titles, such as B.A., M.A., Ph.D., Lover of Mankind, etc. Underneath your name, write your institutional affiliation: Podunk College, Fink University, etc. If you have changed your affiliation since you did the research, list the old affiliation under your name and the new affiliation in a footnote. A dual affiliation is listed under your name only if both institutions contributed financially to the study. If you are unaffiliated with any institution, list your city and state.

ABSTRACT

The abstract summarizes your paper in 100 to 175 words. The abstract, like the title, should be self-explanatory and self-contained, since it is also used for indexing by information-retrieval networks. The abstract should include *(a)* the major hypotheses, *(b)* a summary of the method, including a description of the materials, apparatus, subjects, design, and procedure, *(c)* a synopsis of the main results (including significance levels for statistical tests), and *(d)* the conclusions drawn from the results. Do not include in the abstract any information that is not included in the body of the paper. Since you will not know until you are done with the outline what information you will include, you are well advised to defer writing the abstract until after you have otherwise completed the outline, or even the paper itself.

Remember that most people will read your abstract only if your title interests them, and will read your article only if your abstract interests them. It is therefore essential that the abstract interest your reader. You can interest the reader by showing that the problem is an important one, that your hypotheses about the problem are insightful ones, and that you will test these hypotheses in a convincing way.

INTRODUCTION

The introduction orients the reader to the research. In the paper, it does not receive a heading, since its function is obvious. It should answer four basic questions:

(1) What previous research led up to your research?

(2) What does your research add to this previous research?

(3) Why is the addition made by your research important or interesting?

(4) How is the addition made?

The introduction usually opens with a brief review of the literature most pertinent to your research. A lengthy literature review is inappropriate, except, sometimes, for theses and course assignments. If a voluminous literature exists on the topic, cite a literature review to which the reader can refer for further information if it is wanted. Assume in your review, however, that the reader is familiar with the general area of research. The reader's main interest is in what you have to contribute. He or she is interested in the previous literature only as it relates directly to your contribution.

Once you have told the reader what is already known, you must relate what still needs to be known, i.e., what you intend to find out. Tell the reader not only what you intend to contribute, but also what the nature of the contribution is. Does your research resolve an issue that has been unresolved in the past? Or does it deal with an issue that others have not thought about? Or does it attempt to correct an artifact in previous investigations? This information will give the reader a good idea of what you view as the purpose of your study.

Next, you should show the reader that the contribution is a potentially interesting or important one. Why have people paid attention to this particular issue? Or why is this new issue one that people should pay attention to? Or does an artifact in previous experimental research really undermine conclusions that previous investigators have drawn? Remember that a major purpose of the introduction is to interest the reader in your paper, and that your explanation of why your study is potentially important can motivate the reader either to continue the article or to toss it aside.

Finally, you should tell the reader how you intend to make your contribution. Sketch your experimental design, leaving a detailed description for the *Design* section later in the paper. Show how your design relates to the theoretical issues you address. It is important to convince your reader at this point that your experiment actually does test the hypothesis you want to investigate.

METHOD

The *Method* section tells the reader how the experiment was conducted. You should include just enough information so that the reader could replicate your study. If you include less information, other investigators will be unable to verify your results. If you include more information, you risk boring and possibly losing the reader in needless detail. When you are uncertain as to whether a piece of information is essential, it is better to err in the direction of including too much rather than too little.

The section describing method is usually divided into a number of subsections. Although use of these subsections is optional, it usually simplifies and clarifies the presentation for the reader. The subsections most often used are *Materials, Apparatus, Subjects, Design,* and *Procedure,* although not necessarily in that order. Use the order that best conveys the methods used in your particular experiment.

Materials. You should describe in this subsection the stimulus materials used in the experiment. Sufficient detail should be given so that the reader could generate the same or equivalent stimuli. If the stimuli are unconventional, you might reproduce examples in a table or figure.

Apparatus. The apparatus used in the experiment should be described in this subsection. Present a general description of the apparatus, including any details that might affect the outcome of the experiment. If the apparatus is a standard piece of manufactured equipment, the name and model number will substitute for most details, since the reader can then learn the details from the manufacturer. If the apparatus is unusual, you might want to photograph it and present it as a figure. This entire subsection can be omitted if no apparatus is used.

Subjects. You should describe in this subsection *(a)* the total number of subjects, *(b)* the number of subjects receiving each treatment, *(c)* the population from which the subjects were drawn, *(d)* how subjects were selected, and *(e)* the circumstances under which the subjects participated (e.g., for $2 pay, for course credit, as a favor to the experimenter, etc.). In describing the subject population, include any details that might affect the outcome of the experiment—sex, age, education, etc. The nature of the experiment will determine what other attributes of the subjects might be relevant.

Design. This subsection should include a description of *(a)* the independent variable(s), *(b)* the dependent variable(s), *(c)* the various experimental and control groups and how they were constituted, and *(d)* the way in which subjects were assigned to groups. Be sure to indicate which variables were between-subjects and which within-subjects. This section is sometimes omitted, with the relevant information divided among the other sections. I prefer to include the section, since it provides the reader with a compact overview of the way in which the experiment was put together.

Procedure. This subsection should describe what happened to the subjects in the experimental sessions from the time they walked in to the time they walked out. A chronological account is usually best. Paraphrase directions to subjects, unless they were unconventional, in which case you might want to present them verbatim. Since you assume that your readers have a general knowledge of the relevant literature, you can also assume that they are familiar with standard testing procedures. Therefore, describe such procedures more generally, always being sure to include any details that plausibly might affect the outcome of the experiment.

RESULTS

This section should include *(a)* descriptive statistics, which summarize the data in a readily comprehensible form, and *(b)* inferential statistics, which test the likelihood that the obtained results were not due to chance. If you plan to present a large number of results, divide this section into subsections. The particular subsections used will depend upon the nature of the experiment.

As in the previous sections, you should make an effort to report the right amount of information, neither underreporting nor overreporting your results. And as in the previous sections, it is usually better to report a result if you are uncertain whether to include it. The criteria you should follow are to report *(a)* all data that are directly relevant to your hypotheses, and *(b)* other data that may be peripheral to your hypotheses, but are of particular interest in their own right. Do not present data for individual subjects unless *(a)* you used an $N = 1$ (single-subject) design, *(b)* the individual data show trends that are masked in the group data, or *(c)* your hypotheses are relevant to each individual's data rather than to the group data.

The order in which results are reported is of critical importance. Authors often report first those results that are of most interest or relevance to the hypotheses being tested. Less interesting or relevant results are reported later. You may wish to report first a general conclusion or interpretation, followed by some descriptive statistics that support your assertion, followed only at the end by the inferential statistics that buttress the conclusion. This style of presentation often makes for more interesting reading than a mélange of facts and statistics, followed by an obscurely placed conclusion that the bored reader may never even reach, having given up on your article pages before.

It is often convenient to summarize your data in the form of one or more tables or figures. In planning tables and figures, keep in mind that *(a)* you should not repeat in the text information that is contained in tables and figures, and *(b)* tables and figures should be largely self-explanatory, although you should certainly discuss them in the text. Two more considerations are relevant, but only if you plan to submit a paper to a journal: *(a)* large numbers of tables and figures are discouraged (because they are expensive to reproduce in journals), and *(b)* one or two sentences can often summarize data that initially seem to require a table or figure.

In deciding between presentation of data in a table versus a figure, you face a tradeoff. On the one hand, figures tend to give the reader a better global sense of the data; on the other hand, tables convey information to the reader more precisely. In general, tables are preferred, but your own judgment of what best conveys your message should be the arbiter of how the data are presented.

In reporting tests of statistical significance (this paragraph may be skipped by those unfamiliar with such tests), include *(a)* the name of the test, *(b)* the value of the test statistic, *(c)* the degrees of freedom (if relevant), and *(d)* the significance level of the test. Readers should also be informed whether or not the test is directional, and what the direction of the effect was. Assume that your reader has a knowledge of basic statistics, but describe briefly the assumptions and theory underlying unconventional tests, giving if possible a reference to which the reader can refer. Do not infer that a result is due to the experimental treatment if the significance level is marginal. Such results are best attributed to chance.

DISCUSSION

This section should include *(a)* an explanation of how well your data fit your original hypotheses, *(b)* a statement of your conclusions, and *(c)* a discussion of theoretical, and, if relevant, practical implications of the results.

You should open the discussion with a general statement of how well the data fit your hypotheses. If the data fit your hypotheses, your task is straightforward. If the data do not fit your hypotheses, then you can approach the data from either of two angles. One angle is an acceptance of the data as uninterpretable; the other angle is an interpretation of the data as fitting hypotheses different from those you originally suggested. In either case, you should be as clear in describing lack of fit as you are in describing fit.

If your data are uninterpretable or only partially interpretable, say so. Convoluted explanations of unexpected data are easily recognized as rationalizations of failures. If you have good reason to believe that some aspect of your experiment was responsible for the uninterpretable results, say so briefly and let matters stand there. Do not, however, waste space listing possible reasons for the uninterpretable results: Such lists can go on forever, and are boring to read.

If your data are unexpected but interpretable, it is permissible to interpret them in light of new, reformulated hypotheses. You must make clear, however, that your explanation is *post hoc* and speculative. There is a fine line between reformulation of hypotheses and empty rationalization, so you must convince your reader that your *post hoc* explanation provides a compelling account of the data.

After you have discussed the fit of your data to the original hypotheses, and any new hypotheses you might have, a concise statement of your conclusions should be presented. Since the conclusions are the major message of your paper, you should phrase them with great care, thereby assuring that the reader will interpret them as you intended.

Finally, you should discuss theoretical and possibly practical implications of the results. If you have drawn conclusions different from your original hypotheses, you might suggest ways in which these conclusions could be verified in future research. Do not merely say, however, that future research will be needed to clarify the issues, without giving the reader any inkling of what form this research might take. Every reader knows that more research can be done on any topic. What the reader wants to learn from you is what direction this research should take.

AN ALTERNATIVE: RESULTS AND DISCUSSION

The *Results* and *Discussion* sections are sometimes combined into one section called *Results and Discussion,* especially when each section is relatively short. I recommend this combination even when the individual sections are not short. The problem with a *Results* section standing by itself is that it is difficult to follow and makes for dry reading. The reader is confronted with masses of statistics without being told what the statistics mean or why they are important. Meaningful discussion is deferred until later.

Reconsider our discussion in the previous chapter of thematic versus nonthematic organization. In the present context, one's choices are these:

NONTHEMATIC ORGANIZATION	THEMATIC ORGANIZATION
III. Results	III. Results and Discussion
A. Presentation of Result A	A. Result A
B. Presentation of Result B	1. Presentation
C. Presentation of Result C	2. Discussion
IV. Discussion	B. Result B
A. Discussion of Result A	1. Presentation
B. Discussion of Result B	2. Discussion
C. Discussion of Result C	C. Result C
	1. Presentation
	2. Discussion

In the format on the left, the reader will almost certainly have to refer back to the results from the discussion, unless the results are re-presented in the *Discussion* section, an undesirable redundancy. The reader is unlikely to remember all the results from the *Results* section because they are presented in an unmotivated fashion with no interpretation to make them meaningful.

In the format on the right, there is no need for backward page turning. The results are discussed as they are presented, so that the reader can understand why they are important when they are presented. He or she does not have to wait until later to discover why the author bothered to present those particular results and not others. Consequently, he or she can form a more integrated and coherent representation of the author's results-discussion package.

If the thematic organization on the right is easier to follow than the nonthematic organization on the left, why has the organization on the left been the more widely used? I suspect it is because of a tacit fear that in a joint presentation of results and discussion, the discussion will somehow contaminate the results: Combining the sections will result in a blurring of the distinction between objective and subjective information. This argument, although understandable, is weak. Even a slightly skilled writer can interweave data and discussion of the data in a way that makes clear the distinction between the two. A writer can, of course, be dishonest, and try to pass off his or her opinions as facts. But such a writer can distort his or her data regardless of the way in which the paper is organized.

Regardless of which organization one chooses, related results may be presented and discussed in clusters to increase the meaningfulness of the presentation. For example, Results A and B might be clustered together in the following ways:

NONTHEMATIC ORGANIZATION	THEMATIC ORGANIZATION

III. Results
    A. Presentation of Result Cluster (A,B)
    B. Presentation of Result C
IV. Discussion
    A. Discussion of Result Cluster (A,B)
    B. Discussion of Result C
	III. Results and Discussion
	    A. Result Cluster (A,B)
	      1. Presentation
	      2. Discussion
	    B. Result C
	      1. Presentation
	      2. Discussion

REFERENCE NOTES

This section lists citations to work in progress, personal communications, technical reports, papers presented at meetings, symposia, etc. The format for the notes is discussed in Chapter 6.

REFERENCES

The references provide a complete list of the sources you cite in your paper. The format of the references is the same as for the author cards (see Chapter 2), and is discussed further in Chapter 6. Be sure your references are accurate. Incorrect citations are a disservice to readers and show sloppy scholarship.

APPENDIX

An appendix is rarely used in psychological papers, although it is valuable in certain cases. It is appropriate for *(a)* computer programs designed explicitly for your research, unavailable elsewhere, and possibly valuable to others, *(b)* unpublished tests, *(c)* mathematical proofs that are relevant to your paper but would distract the reader if included in the text, and *(d)* lists of stimulus materials, if the materials are unusual or particularly important to your conclusions (*Publication Manual of the American Psychological Association,* 1974). The appendix should be included only if it is especially enlightening or helpful in enabling others to replicate your study.

ORDER OF SECTIONS

Once you are ready to write your paper in final form, you should order the sections in the following way:

(1) Title page (including your name and affiliation)
(2) Abstract
(3) Text
(4) Reference notes
(5) References
(6) Footnotes
(7) Tables (one table per page)
(8) Figure captions
(9) Figures (one figure per page)

This ordering is to facilitate editing and printing. It is not the order in which the various parts will appear. Pages should be numbered consecutively using arabic numerals, beginning with the abstract. Place page numbers in the upper right corner of each page. Immediately above the page number, write the first few words of your title, or the whole title if the title is short. This way, the pages can be returned to a manuscript in case they are temporarily misplaced.

The ordering above applies to papers written for submission to journals. For course papers, the following exceptions should be noted. First, footnotes usually should be placed at the bottom of the page on which they are cited. Second, tables and figures should be placed near where they are cited in the text rather than at the end. Third, figure captions should be placed immediately below the appropriate figures rather than in a separate section.

Once you have finished ordering and numbering your pages, the paper is completed. You are ready to hand it in or send it off.

4

Rules for Writing the Psychology Paper

Rule #1: *Your writing should interest, inform, and persuade your reader.* Psychological writing should not be dull or stuffy. You must interest your reader in your paper; otherwise, the reader will find something else to do. Even teachers reading course papers will often read boring papers more quickly and less carefully than they will read interesting papers. Although you can lose your reader at any time, the major decision points for the reader are the title, abstract, and introduction.

The optimal title is one that concisely informs the reader of what the article is about. Such a title will minimize the number of people who start the article only to find that the topic doesn't interest them, and maximize the number of people who start the article because the topic does interest them. The abstract should summarize the article and at the same time convey to the reader why the topic, hypotheses, and results are of theoretical or practical interest. The introduction should further motivate the reader by pointing out why the research is a necessary next step in putting together the pieces of an as yet unsolved puzzle. The reader should finish the introduction believing that you have *(a)* put together one or more pieces of the puzzle, and *(b)* pointed the way for further pieces to be put together. This second accomplishment is as important as the first. No one likes to come to the end of an article only to find that the research has hit a dead end.

The best way to inform your reader is to tell him what he is likely to want to know—no more and no less. Experienced writers acquire a knack for knowing what to include and what not to include. Ask yourself which points are central to your main arguments, and which are peripheral details possibly of interest to you but not to your reader.

The major means of persuasion is tight logic. Tight logic is more convincing to readers of psychological papers than are rhetorical devices. Remember that you must sell your ideas but not oversell them, and that you must be persuasive without being condescending. In attacking alternative positions, stick to substance, avoiding *ad hominem* or irrelevant attacks. (Anyone who disagrees with this advice doesn't know what he's talking about!)

Rule #2: *Write for your reader.* Writing for your reader means keeping in mind four things. First, take into account the extent of his or her technical vocabulary. Terms that are familiar to professional psychologists may be unfamiliar to members of a general audience. Even within the field of psychology, specialists in different fields have different technical vocabularies. Whenever you can replace a complicated word with a simple word, do it. If you must use technical words, define them. It is most annoying to find a technical term used repeatedly without first having been defined. Second, maintain a level of formality in your writing that is appropriate for your audience. A book addressed to students (like this book) can be more informal than a book addressed to professional psychologists. Remember, though, that more formal writing need not and should not be stilted. Formality is not a substitute for readability. Third, include only those details that are appropriate for your audience. Readers of a popular journal such as *Psychology Today* will probably be less interested in methodological and statistical details than will readers of the scholarly journal, *Psychological Review*.

Fourth, avoid abbreviations. They can be annoying, and often interfere with the reader's comprehension of the text. (QED!)

Rule #3: *Write clearly.* You know an unclear sentence when you read it. Why, then, don't authors know unclear sentences when they write them? A major reason is their personal involvement in their own work. If an author omits or poorly describes certain details, he or she can subconsciously insert or clarify them. Since the reader does not share the author's cognitive structure, he or she cannot do the same. A large amount of unclear writing would never pass beyond the author's eyes if every author were willing to reread his or her papers in the role of a naive reader. A major reason for lack of clarity in writing is an author's unwillingness to go back over what has been written and rewrite it. One reason for this unwillingness is a delusion that the reader won't notice an unclear sentence. The writer hopes that the imperfections in his or her writing will pass by the reader unnoticed. Unfortunately, the typical outcome is the opposite of what the writer hopes for. The reader stumbles over the unclear sentence, and then rereads it, trying to make sense of it. Instead of the sentence blending into the background, it sticks out like a sore thumb. If there are enough unclear sentences, what started out as a temporary confusion may become a permanent one. Hence, do not succumb to the delusion that you will get away with poor writing. Assume that your reader is as likely to detect an unclear sentence as you are to write one. (For the ideation of unclarity is the worst form of self-indulgence, and an ideological facsimile!)

Rule #4: *Eliminate unnecessary redundancy.* Elimination of redundancy from a paper is a difficult task, because one is never certain of how much redundancy should be eliminated. On the one hand, redundancy can reinforce your points. Readers may comprehend the second time a point that had eluded them the first time. On the other hand, redundancy can obscure your points. When a paper is highly redundant and the reader becomes aware of its redundancy, he or she may start reading the paper more quickly and less carefully, assuming that much of what he or she reads, he or she will have read before and will read again. The reader assumes that if he or she doesn't quite understand a point the first time, he or she will have another chance when the author repeats the point in a slightly different way. The reader may then fail to understand the point because it is not in fact presented again, or because its second presentation is no more enlightening than was the first.

Because redundancy is a double-edged sword, you are better off attaining emphasis through other means. There are three alternative means you can use. First, you can discuss in more detail the points you wish to emphasize. Instead of repeating the points several times at different places in the paper, you give them additional space the first time you make them. Second, you can make important points at strategic places in the paper. People tend to remember best what they read at the beginning or the end of a paper. Third, you can state explicitly that one or more points are of special importance, and thus merit more careful attention. It may be obvious to you which points are your important ones, but it may not be obvious to your reader. Simply telling the reader which points are important can help guide his or her attention in an optimal way.

Writers usually find it much easier to spot redundancy in others' writing than in their own, because they have difficulty distinguishing what they have thought about from what they have written about. They may repeat a point for a second or third time, unaware that they have made the point before. Even in rereading their work, they may have trouble distinguishing their thoughts from their writing. It is therefore a good idea to have someone else read your paper, deliberately seeking out repetitious material.(Since other people usually will not have thought about your topic in the same way you have, they are more likely to recognize redundancy, repetition, reiteration, rehashing, restating, and duplication!)

Rule #5: *Avoid digressions.* Papers are usually difficult enough to follow without the added encumbrance of digressions. Digressions lead the reader away from the main points of your paper. Once the reader's attention is diverted from the main points, there is always a risk that his or her attention will never find its way back to the main points. Occasionally, a digression may be needed to clarify a point. Minor digressions of this kind can be incorporated into footnotes. Major digressions can be incorporated into an appendix. But keep the digressions out of the basic text, where they will distract the reader unnecessarily. (It's off the subject, but all this reminds me about a joke I heard. Two guys walk into a bar, and the first one says . . .)

Rule #6: *Don't overexplain.* Students learning how to write psychology papers often explain too much. This problem is especially apparent in their *Method* sections. A student doing a simple free-recall experiment can end up explaining *(a)* why he or she used visual rather than auditory presentation of words, *(b)* why he or she used nouns instead of other parts of speech, *(c)* why he or she used 18-word lists rather than lists of some other length, *(d)* why he or she presented words at a rate of one word per second rather than some other rate, etc. Assume that readers of your paper (if they are professionals) are familiar with standard procedures, and will be interested only in explanations of nonstandard ones. Exclusive use of people's names, for example, would be nonstandard in a free-recall experiment.

The same warning is relevant to the presentation and discussion of results. If your experiment has only a few results, then you need not select among them. If your experiment has many results, or if you have analyzed the same data in many different ways, select the important results or analyses and concentrate on those. Your selection procedure must be honest: It would be unethical and unscientific to report and discuss only those results that support your hypotheses. The importance of a result should not be determined by its fit to your preconceived notions. (All of this will become clearer when I write my 1000-page tome on how to avoid overexplanation!)

Rule #7: *Avoid overstatement.* Scientific writing should be conservative in its claims. By overstating your case, you undermine your credibility and put your reader on guard. Once on guard, the reader may cease to accept at face value anything you say. Consider, for example, the psychological phenomenon of writing a letter of recommendation for an undergraduate applying to graduate school, or for a graduate student applying for a job. On the one hand, you want to do what you can to assure that a good student obtains the best possible placement. On the other hand, you know that if your claims sound extravagant, you run the risk of damaging your case. Hoping that the major strengths will sell the candidate, writers of letters frequently look for minor weaknesses in their candidates so that their letters will appear impartial. Persons writing and reading letters know that some letter writers have reputations for writing inflated letters, and, as a result, their letters are taken less seriously than the letters of others with higher credibility. The same reputations can be acquired by writers of psychology papers. Someone who is known to overstate his or her case will find others taking his or her claims less seriously than they would have taken the identical claims coming from someone else. (Anyone caught overstating his or her case ought certainly be hanged on the spot!)

Rule #8: *Avoid unnecessary qualifiers.* Qualifiers serve a useful purpose when they honestly limit the scope of a statement. If, for example, only some subjects showed the effect of a certain treatment, then the effect of the treatment should be qualified as limited only to those subjects. Qualifiers serve no purpose, however, if they do not honestly limit scope. A *somewhat* noticeable tremor is not distinguishably different from a noticeable tremor; a *rather* loud pulse is not distinguishably different from a loud pulse. The use of *somewhat* and *rather* in the above contexts draws life from the prose without giving anything in return. In using qualifiers such as *somewhat, rather, mostly, largely, for the most part,* etc., check that they make an honest addition to the sentence. If they don't, throw them out.

Sometimes authors use qualifiers to hedge their bets. Because psychology is an inductive science, proceeding from the specific to the general, psychologists can never draw conclusions with certainty. Psychologists may therefore express their uncertainty by qualifying their conclusions. For example, suppose that in a series of experiments, a psychologist finds that recall of a list of words always increases with practice. He or she concludes that "at least under some circumstances, certain subjects tend to recall more words after more free-recall trials." The qualifications are correct: There are indeed circumstances under which recall will not improve with practice; there are some subjects who will not show increasing recall over trials (e.g., dead ones); and since a given subject's recall may occasionally decrease from one trial to the next (if only by chance), one is safe in referring to a *tendency* toward increasing recall. The author's successive qualifications, however, have left his statement moribund, and have not told the reader anything he or she doesn't already know. Had the author simply stated that "the results indicate that free recall increases over trials," he or she would have made the point without bogging the reader down in excess verbiage. (For the most part, it is usually true that in most cases, absolutely unnecessary qualifiers can often impede communication!)

Rule #9: *Use the precise word.* In the course of writing your paper, you will probably find yourself occasionally stumbling over words, unable to choose a word that expresses the precise meaning you want to convey. Do not settle for an approximate word when a precise word is available. While writing, have available both a dictionary and a thesaurus, so that you can search for the optimal word. Settle for a suboptimal one only if you are unable to find the optimal one after diligent searching. (It is to your advance to alleviate use of ill-chosen words!)

Rule #10: *Prefer simpler to more complicated words.* The main purpose of writing is communication, and simpler words usually communicate more effectively than complicated ones. The reaction of a reader coming across a complicated word he or she doesn't know is not awe for the writer's vocabulary, but annoyance that communication has broken down. The reaction of a reader coming across a complicated word that he or she knows doesn't fit the context in which it is being used is often one of even greater annoyance. Every year, I have at least one student who seems to write papers not to communicate thoughts but to communicate the extent of his or her vocabulary. More often than not, this communication is unsuccessful: The student misuses complicated words. The most important decision regarding words is always to use the one that best expresses your meaning. (If you find that two words express your meaning equally well, use the simpler one, not the more reticular one!)

Rule #11: *Use concrete words and examples.* Much psychological writing is of necessity abstract. Whenever you have a choice, though, between an abstract and a concrete word, choose the concrete one. People will understand you better. When taking your reader through an abstract argument, use examples. If the argument is a long one, don't wait until the end to supply the example. The reader may have gotten lost in your argument a long time before, so that in reading your example he will have to go back through the argument anyway. Your argument will be clearer if you interweave your example(s) with the argument, alternating between the abstract and the concrete. The reader will then be able to understand your argument as he reads it, rather than when (or if) he rereads it. (Indeed, this paragraph would have been clearer if it had provided an example of what it was talking about!)

Rule #12: *Prefer simpler to more complicated sentences.* Sentence structure is largely a matter of style, and you should write in a style comfortable to you. Some master writers, like Hemingway, preferred short sentences; others, like Faulkner, preferred long sentences. The advantages of short sentences, from a journalistic point of view, are that they are *(a)* easier to understand and *(b)* less likely to contain errors of grammar or diction. When you find yourself becoming bogged down in a complicated construction, try to restate in two or more sentences what you had planned to state in one. You will probably find that you are able to say better what you wanted to say. (Having thought about this, you will realize as you read this sentence at the end of the paragraph why complexity in an already long sentence creates bewilderment!)

Rule #13: *Use the active voice.* Use of the impersonal third person in psychological articles encourages overuse of the passive voice. Psychology papers are replete with expressions like *It was found, It can be concluded, The tests were administered, The subjects were told, The session was completed,* etc. Expressions stated in the passive voice are harder to read and make for duller reading than expressions stated in the active voice. Whenever you use a passive construction, try to restate it as an active one. (Although it will be found that this cannot always be done by you, it will be appreciated by your reader, whose understanding of your prose will be enhanced!)

Rule #14: *Prefer affirmative to negative constructions.*
Psychologists have established that negative constructions are
harder to understand than affirmative ones (Clark & Chase,
1972). Your writing will therefore be easier to understand if
you use affirmative rather than negative constructions
wherever possible. In some cases, you will have a choice
between an implicit and an explicit negation. For example, you
might say either that "Writers should avoid negative constructions" or that "Writers should not use negative constructions." Similarly, you might say either that "Six children
were absent from school the day the testing took place" or that
"Six children were not present in school the day the testing
took place." Implicit negations like the first example in each
pair are easier to understand than explicit negations (Clark,
1973), and hence are preferred. (Wherever possible, do not fail
to avoid explicit negations!)

Rule #15: *Avoid dangling constructions.* Dangling constructions make sentences ambiguous, including this one.
The preceding sentence is ambiguous because it is not clear
whether *one* refers to dangling constructions or to sentences.
The source of the ambiguity is the phrase *including this one,*
which dangles at the end of the sentence. Suppose a *Method*
section informs you that "the subjects were falsely debriefed
by the confederates after they finished their task." You cannot
be certain whether *they* and *their* refer to the subjects or to the
confederates. This sentence could be improved by eliminating
the dangling construction. Depending upon who finished the
task, the author might write either *(a)* "after they finished their
task, the confederates falsely debriefed the subjects," or *(b)*
"after they finished their task, the subjects were falsely
debriefed by the confederates." Consider another example
from a *Discussion* section: "The results would have been more
easily interpretable if all the subjects had answered all the
questions affirmatively, not just the first five." In this

sentence, it is not clear whether just the first five subjects answered all the questions affirmatively, or whether all the subjects answered just the first five questions affirmatively. The sentence should be rewritten in one of two ways, depending upon the author's intent: *(a)* "The results would have been more easily interpretable if all the subjects, not just the first five, had answered all the questions affirmatively," or *(b)* "The results would have been more easily interpretable if all the subjects had answered all the questions, not just the first five, affirmatively."

Rule #16: *Avoid participles without referents.* Suppose you read in a paper that "the rat was found dead while cleaning the cage." You probably would be correct to assume that an experimenter or technician, not the dead rat, cleaned the cage. The sentence is ambiguous, however, because it lacks a referent for the participle. Less extreme examples of participles without referents abound in students' writing. Consider the following sentence from a *Method* section: "While monitoring the subject's heartbeat, adrenalin was injected into the subject's left arm." The sentence is unacceptable because it does not state who monitored the subject's heartbeat. Obviously, it wasn't the adrenalin that did the monitoring. But who did? The sentence should be revised to read, "While monitoring the subject's heartbeat, the experimenter injected adrenalin into the subject's left arm." In general, if you use active constructions when you use participles, you will eliminate participles without referents.

Rule #17: *Avoid pronouns without antecedents.* Students learn this rule early in their schooling, and yet they continue to violate it, usually in subtle ways. For example, many students will not recognize the following statement from a *Method* section as ungrammatical: "After the subject's task was completed, he was free to leave." To whom does *he* refer? Obviously not to *task*, but there is no other noun in the sentence, and the antecedent of a pronoun must be a noun. The author could reword the statement to say, "After the subject's task was completed, the subject was free to leave," or better, "After the subject completed the task, he was free to leave."

A possessive pronoun needs an antecedent as much as any other pronoun. Consider, for example, a slight variant of an earlier sentence: "While monitoring the subject's heartbeat, the experimenter injected adrenalin into his left arm." The grammatical antecedent for *his* is *experimenter,* although it is obvious that the author intended otherwise. The author should rephrase the sentence: "While monitoring the subject's heartbeat, the experimenter injected adrenalin into the subject's left arm."

Rule #18: *Avoid use of the indefinite* this. A common problem in student writing is use of the word *this* without a definite antecedent. You will find this even in otherwise well-written prose, as, for example, in this sentence. The first use of *this* is indicative of sloppy prose. Note that there are two possible antecedents of *this, problem* and *use of the word* this *without a definite antecedent.* The ambiguity is eliminated by changing *this* from a pronoun to an adjective: "You will find this problem even in otherwise well-written prose."

Rule #19: *Avoid split infinitives.* Split infinitives seem to evoke two reactions. Some people use them regularly, and barely notice when they read them. Other people never use them, and wince every time they see or hear them. Usually, split infinitives make sentences less graceful without adding any clarity. To carefully weigh the evidence is the same as to weigh the evidence carefully, but the latter way of expressing the idea is more readable than the former. If the adverb with which you want to split the infinitive seems to fit nowhere else, consider rewriting the sentence in a different way. (Try to always follow this advice!)

Rule #20: *Use summary statements.* Psychologists frequently divide long papers into sections and subsections. It is often helpful to include one or two brief summary statements at the end of each section, or at the end of a long argument. Such statements increase comprehensibility at very little cost in additional space. Summaries help the reader *(a)* quickly absorb the main point of each section as he or she completes it, and *(b)* keep track of where he or she is. A long summary in the middle of a paper is unnecessary and inadvisable, since it is redundant with the abstract and possibly the conclusions. (To summarize, a summary at this point in the chapter is unnecessary!)

Rule #21: *Use transitions.* Have you ever noticed that some people write clear sentences, and yet their writing nevertheless appears disjointed? A common cause of disjointed and choppy writing is missing transitions between ideas. Missing transitions are sometimes caused by careless thinking: The writer goes from step A to step C without thinking of the necessary intervening step B. More often, though, missing transitions are caused by quick thinking: The writer thinks faster than he writes. As the writer is writing sentence A, the writer is already thinking about sentence B. By the time the writer finishes writing sentence A, he or she has started thinking about sentence C, and so proceeds to write sentence C, forgetting to insert the necessary transitional sentence B. No matter how clearly sentences A and C are stated, the reader will pause in reading sentence C, wondering whether he or she missed something in sentence A, or even in some sentence further back. Missing transitions can be inserted if you reread your paper, checking carefully whether each sentence follows logically from the sentence immediately preceding it. (The price of rice also increased in China during this past year!)

Rule #22: *Place yourself in the background.* There was a time when it was considered bad form for the writer to place himself or herself anywhere near the foreground of a paper. Writers avoided first person references at all costs. When strictures against first person references started to ease, single writers often started referring to themselves as *we,* even if they were sole authors of papers. Today, references to oneself as *we* are discouraged. If you are sole author of a paper and use the expression *we,* you should use it only to refer to yourself and your readers, not just to yourself. If you mean *I,* say *I.* Overuse of the first person singular, however, tends to distract the reader, calling attention to you rather than to what you are saying. Stay in the background, therefore, surfacing only when you have good reason to draw attention to yourself, e.g., in emphasizing that an idea is your own speculation, rather than a conclusion closely following from a set of data. (We cannot emphasize this point more strongly!)

Rule #23: *Cite sources as well as findings.* When you cite a finding, cite its source. There are four reasons why you should supply this information. First, the reader can check whether you have cited the source accurately. He or she may doubt the finding, and want to verify that you properly cited it. Second, the reader can check whether the source is credible. If you merely cite a finding, the reader has no way of checking the quality of the evidence in support of that finding. Third, the reader can learn about a reference that he or she may have been unaware of, and that he or she then wants to read. Fourth, you show your reader that you are familiar with the literature on your topic, thereby increasing your own credibility as a source of information. (In fact, research has shown that citing sources of research findings does improve credibility!)

Rule #24: *Proofread your paper.* I would estimate that fewer than one-half the papers I receive have been proofread by their authors. Fewer than one-quarter are proofread carefully. I think that students often fail to proofread their work because they are afraid they won't like what they read. But other readers of your paper will like it even less if they have to put up with errors that the author easily could have corrected. I cannot emphasize enough the importance of proofreading. The time it takes to proofread a paper is a small fraction of the time it takes to write the paper. And there is probably no other thing you can do in as little time that will as much improve others' evaluations of your work.

The best method of proofreading is to have someone read the text to you from the original, while you check the final typed copy line-by-line. In following the typed text, read only for errors in spelling, punctuation, capitalization, and the like. Do not read for meaning. You should read the paper an additional time to make sure that you have said what you wanted to say, the way you wanted to say it. (Typografikal erors are uneccesary!)

Rule #25: *Request a critical reading of your paper by an adviser or colleague.* Because people are so involved in their own work, they find it much easier to criticize the work of others than to criticize their own work. It is therefore to your advantage to seek the advice of others on any paper you write. When asking someone to read your paper, ask them to read it *critically,* indeed, ruthlessly. It is a common experience for authors to receive compliments from their colleagues on their papers, and then to find them torn to shreds by journal reviewers. One reason for the discrepancy is that colleagues you ask to read your paper may not willingly sacrifice the time or risk the loss of friendship that might be involved in a very critical reading of your work. Encourage your readers to be critical, therefore, perhaps offering your own critical paper-reading services in return.

CHAPTER 5

Commonly Misused Words

This chapter explains the meanings of some of the most commonly misused words in student papers. The chapter is divided into two parts. The first part deals with meanings of nontechnical terms. Strunk and White (1972) provide a longer list, and Fowler (1959) provides a complete dictionary of English usage. The second part of the chapter deals with meanings of technical terms. The psychological dictionaries and encyclopedias described in Chapter 7 provide much more extensive lists of psychological terms.

Nontechnical Terms

(1) *adapt, adopt.* To adapt is to accommodate, to adjust, to bring into correspondence. To adopt is to embrace, to take on, to make one's own.

    (a) Organisms adapt to their environment.

    (b) Children adopt the attitudes of their peers.

(2) *adopt.* See *(1)*.

(3) *affect, effect.* Both words can be used either as nouns or as verbs. An affect is an emotion, or something that tends to arouse an emotion. An effect is a result or outcome of some cause. To affect is to influence, or to have an effect upon something. To effect is to accomplish or to achieve.

    (a) His display of affect in response to the TAT pic-

ture seemed artificial and contrived to gain the psychologist's sympathy.

(b) The effect of the experimental treatment was negligible.

(c) Shoddy procedures affect the outcome of an experiment.

(d) He was able to effect a change in behavior by desensitizing the patient to snakes.

(4) *aggravate, irritate.* To aggravate is to intensify, to heighten, or to magnify. To irritate is to annoy, to inflame, to provoke.

(a) Don't aggravate his frustration by telling him that he answered all the questions incorrectly.

(b) Experimenters who deceive subjects often irritate the subjects.

(5) *allusion.* An allusion is an indirect reference. An explicit statement about *X* is not an allusion to *X*.

(a) The first experimenter made an allusion to a reward for exceptional performance, but he never came out and directly told the subject that the subject would receive a reward.

(b) The second experimenter told the subject he would receive a reward for exceptional performance. (He did not allude to a reward.)

(6) *among, between.* A relation is between two things and among more than two things. The term *between* can be used for a relation involving more than two things if reciprocity is involved in the relation. When in doubt regarding relations among more than two things, use *among.*

(a) The subject had to decide between the button on the left and the button on the right.

(b) The subject had to decide among the left, middle, and right buttons.

(c) The agreement between the three members of the group broke down quickly when the experimental manipulation was introduced.

(7) *amount of, number of.*   An amount of something is a sum total or aggregate. A number of something is a quantity of it. Use *amount of* when dealing with quantities that can't be counted. Use *number of* when dealing with quantities that can be counted. Monetary terms are exceptions to this generalization.

(a) The amount of liquid in the tall jar was the same as the amount in the fat jar.

(b) The number of stimuli was too small.

(c) The subject was dissatisfied with the amount of money he received for participating in the experiment.

(8) *and/or.*   Avoid this expression, which means that a relation is either conjunctive *(and)* or disjunctive *(or).* The expression disrupts the flow of prose, is ambiguous, and often indicates that the author couldn't decide which conjunction to use, so he or she used both simultaneously.

(9) *as to whether.*   Avoid this expression. Say *whether.*

(10) *between.*   See *(6).*

(11) *bring, take.*   To bring something is to carry it toward the speaker or listener. To take something is to carry it away from the speaker or listener.

(a) Take this incomprehensible book back to the library.

(b) Bring me a better book from the library.

(12) *certainly.*   Use the word *certainly* only if you mean "with 100% probability." Don't use the word loosely to connote near-certainty.

(a) He certainly won't eat his hat.

(13) *compare to, compare with.* To compare to is to point out or emphasize similarities between different things. To compare with is to point out or emphasize differences between similar things.

(a) The student compared the predictions of the continuous learning model to those of the discrete learning model, and showed that they were indistinguishable.

(b) The student compared Freud's conception of the ego with Erikson's conception, and showed that the two conceptions differed in fundamental respects.

(14) *comprise.* To comprise is to consist of or to embrace. This word has the dubious distinction of being misused more often than it is properly used in student papers. A whole comprises its parts; parts constitute (form, or compose) a whole.

(a) This book comprises nine fascinating chapters.

(15) *continual, continuous.* *Continual* means often repeated. *Continuous* means without stop.

(a) Continual interruptions forced the experimenter to terminate the session early.

(b) Continuous background music improved employees' morale.

(16) *continuous.* See *(15)*.

(17) *data.* *Data* is a plural noun, and requires a plural verb. The singular form is *datum.* This form is used infrequently.

(a) The professor's data were far from perfect.

(b) One datum was inconsistent with all the rest.

(18) *different from, different than.* If two things differ, they are different from each other. The expression *different than* is incorrect.

(19) *discover, invent.* To discover something is to find something that was there before. To invent something is to create something new.

(a) No one has discovered a single gene for intelligence.

(b) Some people would like to invent a pill to increase intelligence.

(20) *disinterested, uninterested.* To be disinterested is to be impartial. To be uninterested is to be lacking in interest.

(a) There seem to be few disinterested investigators studying the heritability of intelligence. Most of them have obvious biases.

(b) Psychoanalysts are generally uninterested in stimulus-response explanations of behavior.

(21) *effect.* See *(3)*.

(22) *enormity, enormousness.* The former word refers to extreme wickedness, the latter to extreme size or volume.

(a) The enormity of the tyrant's crimes could not be simulated in an experimentally-controlled setting.

(b) The enormousness of the giant scared the children.

(23) *enormousness.* See *(22)*.

(24) *fact.* A fact should be directly verifiable either empirically or logically. Do not refer to judgments or probable outcomes as facts.

(25) *factor.* Because this word has at least two technical meanings in psychology (see the next section of this chapter), it is best not to use it in a loose, nontechnical sense. Instead of saying, for example, that "several factors contributed to the subject's euphoria," say that "the subject was euphoric for several reasons."

(26) *farther, further.* The word *farther* should be used

to refer to greater distance; the word *further* should be used to refer to greater quantity or time.

   (*a*) Further jokes were to no avail; the subject refused to laugh.

   (*b*) The patient explained to the psychologist that the farther he traveled from his home, the more anxious he felt.

(27) *fewer, less.*   *Fewer* refers to number, *less* to amount or degree.

   (*a*) The patient had fewer nightmares after he began therapy.

   (*b*) The patient's nightmares became less frightening after he began therapy.

(28) *former, latter.*   *Former* refers to the first item in a series, *latter* to the second. These words are applicable when the series consists of just two items, or when a longer series is divided into two parts. In series with more than two items, refer to the endpoints of the series as the first and last items.

   (*a*) The male and female confederates entered the room together, the former carrying a live alligator and the latter carrying a dead rattlesnake.

   (*b*) Of the three people who interviewed for the job, only the first was qualified but only the last was willing to take the job after finding out what it entailed.

(29) *fortuitous, fortunate.*   A fortuitous event is one that occurs by chance. A fortunate event is one that is favored by fortune.

   (*a*) The simultaneous appearance of the two rivals was made to appear fortuitous, but it was in fact contrived.

   (*b*) The appearance of all the subjects at the testing session was most fortunate, because the machine controlling the testing exploded at the end of the session, and thereafter was incapable of further use.

(30) *fortunate.* See *(29)*.

(31) *further.* See *(26)*.

(32) *hopefully.* This word means *full of hope*. It does not mean *it is to be hoped*. Today, this word is more often used incorrectly than correctly.

 (a) He started the experiment hopefully, but ended it discouraged.

(33) *imply, infer.* To imply something is to suggest it indirectly. To infer something is to conclude or deduce it from the information available. The two words are not interchangeable.

 (a) The patient implied that he still felt like strangling anyone who got in his way.

 (b) The therapist thus inferred that the patient was not yet cured.

(34) *infer.* See *(33)*.

(35) *interesting.* This word is overused. Saying that something is interesting is not a substitute for making it interesting.

(36) *invent.* See *(19)*.

(37) *irregardless.* This word does not exist in English. The proper word is *regardless*.

 (a) The rat receives a sugar pellet after pressing the bar, regardless of how long he takes to press it.

(38) *irritate.* See *(4)*.

(39) *its, it's.* The word *its* means *belonging to* or *pertaining to*. The word *it's* means *it is* or *it has*.

 (a) The investigator knew the fear manipulation had failed when the monster shook its tail and the children laughed in response.

(b) After seeing the children's response, the investigator thought to himself: "It's all over."

(40) *latter.* See *(28).*

(41) *lay, lie.* *Lay* and *lie* both have a number of meanings. Confusion regarding which word to use arises from one meaning of each word. For *lay,* this meaning is *to put or place something.* For *lie,* this meaning is *to recline.* The past tense of *lay* is *laid,* and the present perfect is *have laid.* The past tense of *lie* is *lay,* and the present perfect is *have lain.* *Lay* always takes an object; *lie* never does.

(a) (i) When the experimenter enters the room, he lays the booklets on the table.

(ii) The experimenter laid the booklets on the table.

(iii) The experimenter has laid the booklets on the table.

(b) (i) The patient lies down on a couch when he enters the therapist's office.

(ii) The patient lay down on a couch after he entered the therapist's office.

(iii) After the patient has lain down, the therapist begins the session.

(42) *less.* See *(27).*

(43) *lie.* See *(41).*

(44) *literally.* If something is literally true, then it is true in fact. Use *literally* only if you mean it. Do not use the expression *literally true* if you mean figuratively true or almost true.

(45) *number.* See *(7).*

(46) *one.* Do not follow *one* by *his.* Follow it by *one's.*

(a) One must organize one's papers carefully in order for them to communicate effectively.

(47) *only.* Careless placement of *only* in a sentence can change the meaning of the sentence. Place *only* immediately before the word or clause it modifies. Do not say, for example, "I only tested five subjects" if you mean, "I tested only five subjects." Consider how the meaning of a sentence changes, depending upon the placement of *only:*

    (a) Only I will treat the patient in my office tomorrow.

    (b) I only will treat the patient in my office tomorrow.

    (c) I will only treat the patient in my office tomorrow.

    (d) I will treat only the patient in my office tomorrow.

    (e) I will treat the only patient in my office tomorrow.

    (f) I will treat the patient only in my office tomorrow.

    (g) I will treat the patient in only my office tomorrow.

    (h) I will treat the patient in my only office tomorrow.

    (i) I will treat the patient in my office only tomorrow.

    (j) I will treat the patient in my office tomorrow only.

(48) *principal, principle.* Used as an adjective, *principal* means *chief, dominant, main, major.* Used as a noun, it means *a person or thing of importance or rank. Principle* can be used only as a noun, and it refers to *a general truth or law.*

    (a) The principal reason for not scoring the subject's test was that the subject had cheated in answering the last two problems.

    (b) This book presents many principles for writing psychology papers.

(49) *principle.* See *(48).*

(50) *relevant.* Use this word only if you can specify a precise relationship. Do not use it to express a vague connection to everyday life or your own experience, as in "Clinical psychology is relevant." If you make the connection clear, then the word is appropriate:

    (a) Clinical psychology is relevant to everyday life.

(51) *take.* See *(11).*

(52) *that, which.* *That* is used for restrictive clauses, *which* for nonrestrictive clauses. Clauses using *which,* therefore, are surrounded by commas. The use of *which* for *that* is common in psychological (and other) writing, but is inadvisable. Excessive use of *which* makes sentences cumbersome and difficult to read. The advice of Strunk and White (1972) is most appropriate: "The careful writer, watchful for small conveniences, goes *which*-hunting, removes the defining *whiches,* and by doing so improves his work" (p. 53).

(a) The experiment that he designed is a gem. (This sentence tells which experiment is a gem.)

(b) The experiment, which he designed, is a gem. (This sentence tells something about the one experiment in question.)

(53) *try.* Say "try to," not "try and."

(a) Before he showed the picture of the snake to the patient, the therapist told the patient to try to relax.

(54) *uninterested.* See *(20).*

(55) *unique.* Something that is unique is one-of-a-kind. It is not merely unusual or extraordinary. There can be no degrees of uniqueness.

(a) The psychologist employed a unique combination of therapeutic techniques in treating his patients.

(56) *utilize.* *Use* is simpler, and usually serves just as well.

(a) The subject used the process of elimination to answer the multiple-choice test questions.

(57) *which.* See *(52).*

(58) *while.* This word is best used to mean "at the same time that." It is frequently used as a substitute for *whereas, but,* and *although.* The word does not serve well as a substitute, because it is not clear whether the author intends to imply simultaneity. The sentence, "I went east while he went west" is unambiguous if the reader knows that the author uses *while* only to mean *at the same time that.* But if the author sometimes uses *while* to mean *whereas,* the sentence is ambiguous: The reader does not know whether the two individuals went in opposite directions at the same time. Similarly, if "the subject answered test questions while the examiner scored them," the reader will want to infer that answering and scoring occurred simultaneously.

(a) The experimenter appeared nonchalant while the subject finished the task.

(59) *Whom.* This word is often used incorrectly before expressions like *he said,* when *who* should serve as the subject of the verb following the expression.

(a) The graduate student who the professor said would come to Yale went to Squeedunk instead. (*Who* is the subject of *would come.*)

(60) *Whose.* This word can serve as the possessive case of either *who* or *which.* Hence, it can refer to inanimate as well as animate objects.

(a) The subject was upset when the machine whose buttons he pressed disintegrated in less than five seconds.

(b) The experimenter, however, knew whose fault the disintegration was, and had trouble holding back a smile.

Technical Terms

(1) *ability, capacity.* Capacity is innate potential. Ability is developed capacity. One's ability may not reflect one's capacity if environmental circumstances have been unfavorable to the development of that capacity. Only ability can be measured; hence, we cannot assess the degree to which one's ability reflects one's capacity.

(a) The child's test scores indicated only marginal ability to succeed in school work.

(b) The child's unhappy childhood suggested to the psychologist that the child's capacity for school work might not be reflected in his scores on ability tests.

(2) *algorithm, heuristic.* An algorithm is a systematic routine for solving a problem that will eventually solve the problem, even if solution involves consideration of all possible answers to the problem. A heuristic is a short-cut or informal routine for solving a problem that may or may not eventually solve the problem. An algorithm may be slow, but it is guaranteed eventually to reach an answer. A heuristic is relatively fast, but does not guarantee solution. Some problems can be solved only by heuristics. No algorithm is available, for example, that guarantees that a given move in a game of chess is the optimal move.

(a) The subject discovered an algorithm for solving the jigsaw puzzle, but the algorithm required 752,964 arrangements of the pieces of the puzzle to guarantee a solution.

(b) Another subject discovered a heuristic for solving the puzzle that he estimated gave him a 75% chance of solving the puzzle after only 55 arrangements of the pieces.

(3) *anxiety, fear.* Anxiety is a state (or trait) of apprehension or uneasiness with no well-defined object. Fear is a state of apprehension in response to a well-defined threat.

(a) The executive felt a constant sense of anxiety, and yet was unable to pinpoint anything in his environment that threatened his well-being.

(b) The hunter was filled with fear when his rifle failed to fire and the bear started charging toward him.

(4) *applied research, basic research.* Applied research strives for findings of practical value, regardless of whether or not they have theoretical value. Basic research strives for find-

ings of theoretical value, regardless of whether or not they have practical value. Applied research may yield findings of theoretical value, and basic research may yield findings of practical value, although such findings are incidental to the major goals of each type of research.

(a) Research on consumer preferences for different kinds of cosmetic products has been almost exclusively applied research.

(b) Research on serial learning of nonsense syllables has been primarily basic research.

(5) *artificial intelligence, simulation.* Artificial intelligence researchers seek to build machines or instructions for machines that solve in an optimal way problems usually thought to require intelligence. Little or no attempt is made to have these machines or instructions correspond to the human mind or the strategies used by the human mind. Simulation research seeks to build machines or instructions for machines that solve problems in ways analogous to those used by humans. Little or no attempt is made to achieve optimal performance. Indeed, if human performance is suboptimal, then an attempt is made to imitate this suboptimal performance.

(a) Using the techniques of artificial intelligence, the computer scientist was able to program a computer to solve algebra problems far more efficiently than human beings solve them.

(b) The psychologist wrote a simulation program that closely matched the techniques of Algebra I students in solving algebra problems.

(6) *average.* As a statistical term, this word is used in two ways. The more specific way is as a synonym for *mean.* Used in this way, the average is the sum of a set of values divided by the number of values. The more general way is as a generic term for all measures of central tendency (cf. mean,

median, mode). Used in this way, the average is the central value, however defined. In order to avoid confusion, the word *average* is best used only in its more specific meaning.

    (a) The five children taking the test had scores of 2, 4, 4, 6, and 14, for an average of 6.

    (7) *avoidance learning, escape learning.* Avoidance learning is motivated by avoidance of punishment. The learner is punished only if learning does not take place. Escape learning is motivated by escape from punishment. The learner is punished until learning takes place.

    (a) After being suspended from school for a third time, the mischievous child learned not to play practical jokes on his classmates. (This situation provides an example of avoidance learning.)

    (b) The rat learned to jump on the pedestal whenever the floor to his cage was electrified. (This situation provides an example of escape learning.)

    (8) *basic research.* See *(4)*.

    (9) *classical conditioning, operant conditioning.* In classical conditioning, an originally neutral stimulus is repeatedly paired with a stimulus that evokes a certain response. This latter stimulus is called the unconditioned stimulus, or US. The response given to the stimulus is called the unconditioned response, or UR. As a result of the repeated pairing, the originally neutral stimulus eventually starts to evoke the same response as the unconditioned stimulus, even if it is not paired with the US any more. At this point, the originally neutral stimulus becomes a conditioned stimulus, or CS. The response given to this stimulus is called the conditioned response, or CR. In operant conditioning, a learner is rewarded (reinforced) each time a desired response takes place. Eventually, the learned response occurs even without paired presentation of the reward.

(a) Every time the salesman visited his southeast Asian client, the salesman became ill from the change in climate; the salesman was surprised, though, when the client came to visit him and he became sick without exposure to the different climate. (This situation provides an example of classical conditioning.)

(b) As a child, he was given a lollipop every time he took his vitamins without complaining, and as an adult, he continued to take his vitamins without complaining, even though the lollipop no longer accompanied the vitamins. (This situation provides an example of operant conditioning.)

(10) *compulsion, obsession.* A compulsion is an irresistible urge to perform repeatedly a stereotyped act that serves no apparent purpose. An obsession is a recurrent thought that the thinker is powerless to control.

(a) The therapist suggested to the patient that the patient's desire to wash his hands every 15 minutes might be a compulsion rather than a reasonable wish for cleanliness.

(b) As a soldier during the Korean War, he had seen a little girl shot to death on the battlefield. Since then he was obsessed: A vision of the little girl being shot plagued him at least twice every waking hour.

(11) *control group, experimental group.* A control group is one that does not receive the experimental treatment of interest. An experimental group is one that does receive the treatment. The effect of the treatment can then be assessed by comparing performance in the experimental group with that in the control group. The term *experimental group* is sometimes used in a more general sense to refer to any group in an experiment. In order to avoid confusion, the term is better restricted to the more limited, contrastive usage.

(a) Members of the experimental group were told that they had been selected because their teachers had rated them unusually likely to succeed in difficult reasoning tasks.

(b) Members of one control group were told that they had been selected at random, whereas members of a second control group were not told anything about selection procedures. The first group served as a control for telling subjects that they were rated unusually likely to succeed, and the second group served as a control for telling subjects anything at all about selection procedures.

(12) *culture-fair test, culture-free test.* A culture-fair test is one that attempts to minimize the *differential* effects of different cultural experiences upon performance. A culture-free test is one that attempts to minimize the *absolute* effects of any cultural experiences upon performance. Construction of a culture-fair test is a sensible goal, although one that probably only can be approached. Construction of a culture-free test is not a sensible goal, *(a)* because the very act of taking a test is culture-bound, and *(b)* because we have no culture-free baseline against which to assess the success of a culture-free test. In other words, we have no way of knowing what *culture-free* means.

(a) By using only pictures of naturally and commonly occurring objects, the investigator hoped to attain a culture-fair test.

(b) The investigator set out to make a culture-free test by stripping away from his culture-bound test everything that in any way reflected cultural experiences; when he finished his task, he realized he had nothing left.

(13) *culture-free.* See *(12)*.

(14) *deduction, induction.* Deduction is reasoning from the general to the specific. Given general principles, one deduces specific outcomes. A characteristic of deduction is that one can attain certainty in one's conclusions. If the premises are valid and the reasoning correct, then the conclusions must be valid. Mathematical and logical proofs are usually deductive. Induction is reasoning from the specific to the general. Given specific outcomes, one induces general principles. A characteristic of induction is that one can never attain certainty in one's conclusions. One can disconfirm but never confirm with certainty an inductive argument.

(a) From just a few basic axioms, Euclid was able to deduce all the theorems that constitute what we now call Euclidean geometry.

(b) A jeweler observed that all emeralds he had ever seen were green. He induced on the basis of his extensive observations that all emeralds are green, regardless of whether or not he had seen them. He realized, though, that the induction could be disconfirmed by the subsequent appearance of just a single nongreen emerald, but that the induction could not be confirmed because the next emerald he saw might be nongreen.

(15) *delusion, hallucination, illusion.* A delusion is a false belief. A hallucination is a sensory experience in the absence of an appropriate external stimulus. An illusion is a misperception of a stimulus.

(a) The psychologist tried to convince the patient that his belief that his friends were secretly plotting against him was a delusion.

(b) After three days without water in the desert, the explorer saw an oasis ahead; but when he reached the point where he had seen the oasis, and saw only dry sand, he realized he had suffered a hallucination.

(c) The clever student knew that his perception of the train tracks as meeting each other on the horizon was an illusion.

(16) *dependent variable, independent variable.* A dependent variable is one whose value is affected by (is dependent upon) the value of some other variable(s). These other variables, which are the variables under experimental control, are the independent variables.

(a) The dependent variable in the experiment was reaction time to a visually presented stimulus.

(b) The independent variables in the experiment were length of stimulus presentation and clarity of the visual stimulus.

(17) *descriptive statistics, inferential statistics.* Descriptive statistics summarize data. They include indices such as the mean, median, standard deviation, and correlation coefficient. Each of these statistics tells us some important property of the data under consideration. Inferential statistics provide tests of hypotheses about data or simply permit generalizations about populations from sample data. They include such indices as t, z, and F. Each of these statistics is used to test hypotheses about differences between one value (or set of values) and another.

(a) The author first presented descriptive statistics so that his readers could get a feeling for the data.

(b) Then he presented inferential statistics so that readers could see the extent to which the data were consistent with his hypotheses.

(18) *deviation IQ, ratio IQ.* The IQ, or intelligence quotient, was originally conceived of as a ratio of mental age to chronological age. This ratio (or quotient) was soon perceived to have several disadvantages. First, it seemed to assume that mental age kept increasing as long as chronological age increased, whereas in fact mental age increases very slowly after a person reaches a chronological age of 16, and eventually it begins to decrease. Second, the ratio assumed that increases in mental age are continuous in the same way that increases in chronological age are continuous, although the research of Piaget (1952) and others indicates that this is not the case. In order to correct for these undesirable properties of the ratio IQ, deviation IQs were introduced. These IQs are not actually quotients, although the designation "IQ" was retained. The concept of mental age is not used in the calculation of deviation IQs. Instead, the IQs are fixed at a certain mean, usually 100, and a certain standard deviation, usually 15 or 16. IQs are then computed on the basis of each person's standardized deviation from the mean. If the mean IQ is set to 100 and the standard deviation to 15, the deviation IQ is equal to [(Raw Score − Mean Score) / (Standard Deviation)] × 15 + 100.

(a) The child's raw score on the intelligence test was 50. Since the mean on the test was 40, and the standard deviation was 10, his deviation IQ was [(50-40) / 10] × 15 + 100, or 115.

(b) The child's raw score of 50 corresponded to a mental age of 12 years, 0 months. Since his chronological age was 10 years, 0 months, his ratio IQ was (12/10) = 120.

(19) *escape learning.* See *(7)*.

(20) *empiricism, nativism.* Empiricism is a view that behavior is learned primarily as a result of experience. In its extreme form, it claims that all behavior is acquired through experience. Nativism makes the claim that most behavior is innately determined. In its extreme form, it claims that all behavior is innately determined.

(a) Empiricists such as Skinner claim that language acquisition can be explained by operant conditioning.

(b) Nativists such as Chomsky claim that language acquisition can be understood only if one postulates an innate competence for learning (sometimes called a language acquisition device).

(21) *experimental group.* See *(11)*.

(22) *experimental psychology.* This term is used in two different ways. Properly used, it refers to a methodology—the use of experiments to collect data. Thus, psychologists who collect data via experiments are referred to as experimental psychologists. A second and less desirable use of the term is as referring to a substantive area of psychology embracing sensation, perception, learning, memory, and thinking. This latter usage developed because researchers interested in these processes have long (although not always) used experimental methods. Since investigators in other areas of psychology (e.g., personality, social, developmental) may also use experimental methods, the term *experimental psychology* is better used in its first meaning.

(a) Using experimental methods, the investigator concluded that introverts were more likely to complete his boring task than were extraverts.

(23) *extrinsic motivation, intrinsic motivation.* Extrinsic motivation is motivation controlled by the possibilities of reward or punishment other than those directly achieved by engaging in a behavior or by the outcome of that behavior. Intrinsic motivation is motivation controlled by the possibilities of reward or punishment that are achieved directly by engaging in a behavior or by the outcome of that behavior.

(a) The student's motivation to learn geometry was extrinsic: He wanted to receive an A in his geometry course.

(b) His friend's motivation to learn geometry was intrinsic: He enjoyed learning how all of geometry could be deduced from a few simple axioms.

(24) *factor.* This word has two common technical meanings in psychology. First, it can refer to an independent variable in an experiment. A three-factor experiment is one with three independent variables. Second, the word can refer to a mathematical representation of a hypothetical psychological construct. This mathematical representation is obtained through a statistical technique called factor analysis.

(a) The student manipulated two factors in his experiment, attractiveness and sex of the confederate.

(b) According to Spearman's theory of intelligence, intelligence comprises one general factor common to performance on all intellectual tasks and many specific factors, each limited to performance on a single intellectual task.

(25) *fear.* See *(3)*.

(26) *fixation, regression.* Fixation refers to arrested development at some stage, usually a stage earlier than the one an individual should be in. Regression refers to a return to an earlier stage of development.

(a) The five-year-old child's continual sucking of anything he could get into his mouth suggested to the psychologist that the child had fixated at the oral stage of development.

(b) The soldier seemed perfectly normal until he entered the battlefield, at which time he showed regression toward infantile behaviors that he had not exhibited for more than two decades.

(27) *genotype, phenotype.* A genotype is a set of inherited characteristics that may or may not be displayed. A phenotype is the set of characteristics that is displayed.

(a) The woman's phenotype revealed brown eyes.

(b) When the brown-eyed woman had a child with blue eyes, it became apparent that her genotype included the recessive gene for blue eyes as well as the dominant gene for brown eyes.

(28) *hallucination.* See *(15)*.

(29) *heritability.* Heritability is the proportion of the total variance of a trait in a population that is attributable to

genetic differences among individuals in that population. Heritability is thus the ratio of (variance due to genetic causes) / (total variance). (See item 68.)

(a) Height is a characteristic with high heritability, whereas temperament is a characteristic with low heritability.

(30) *identification, imitation.* In identification, a person (often a child) acquires the social role of another person by modeling the behavior of that person. In imitation, the person models the behavior of another person, not necessarily acquiring that person's social role.

(a) Because the man identified with his lazy and irresponsible father, he found himself unable to cope with his family responsibilities.

(b) The young boy often imitated the actions of his mother, but he eventually identified with his father.

(31) *illusion.* See *(15)*.

(32) *imitation.* See *(30)*.

(33) *independent variable.* See *(16)*.

(34) *induction.* See *(14)*.

(35) *inferential statistics.* See *(17)*.

(36) *intrinsic motivation.* See *(23)*.

(37) *latent content, manifest content.* The latent content of a dream is its deeper, hidden meaning. The manifest content of a dream is its apparent meaning.

(a) The manifest content of the dream consisted of the patient's being chased out of a luxurious palace across a moat by an angry older man wielding a big stick.

(b) The psychologist believed the latent content of the dream was sexual, and that the man exhibited through the dream an unresolved Oedipal conflict.

(38) *learning, maturation, performance.* Learning is

often distinguished both from maturation and from performance. Learning is an increment in knowledge that occurs as a result of practice. Maturation is a change in behavior resulting from a growth process that is independent of practice. Performance is overt behavior. Note that learning takes place only with practice; maturation takes place regardless of whether or not it is preceded by practice. Note also that learning may occur without showing itself through a change in performance.

(a) The child repeatedly failed to understand that the amount of liquid in the tall jar was the same as the amount obtained when the contents of the tall jar were poured into the fat jar. Eventually, his cognitive abilities matured to the point at which he could understand the principle of conservation, and thus the equality between the two amounts of liquid.

(b) Although the subject had learned all the words in the list, his recall performance was far from perfect; it was not until the subject was given a test of recognition performance that he showed that he was familiar with all of the words.

(39) *manifest content.* See *(37).*

(40) *maturation.* See *(38).*

(41) *mean, median, mode.* The mean (average) is the sum of a set of values divided by the number of values. The median is the middle value: Half the values are higher and half are lower. The mode is the most frequently occurring value.

(a) The mean of the numbers 2, 2, 4, 6, and 16 is 6.

(b) The median of the numbers 2, 2, 4, 6, and 16 is 4.

(c) The mode of the numbers 2, 2, 4, 6, and 16 is 2.

(42) *median.* See *(41).*

(43) *mode.* See *(41).*

(44) *nativism.* See *(20).*

(45) *nature-nurture.* The nature-nurture distinction refers to the relative proportions of variance in traits or behaviors attributable to heredity *(nature)* versus environment *(nurture).*

(a) In the nature-nurture debate, hereditarians favor nature and environmentalists favor nurture as the primary source of differences in behavior.

(46) *neurosis, psychosis.* A neurosis is a minor disorder in which a person exhibits maladaptive behavior patterns (symptoms) that avoid rather than cope with underlying problems. A psychosis is a major disorder in which a person exhibits severely maladaptive behavior patterns that usually require treatment in a hospital.

(a) The neurotic man counted his money every hour-on-the-hour to make sure it hadn't fallen out of his pocket.

(b) The psychotic man continually saw robbers reaching out to grab his wallet, but when he chased the robbers, they always disappeared into thin air.

(47) *null hypothesis.* The null hypothesis is a hypothesis of no difference. It is not *no* hypothesis.

(a) The investigator's null hypothesis was that the treatment would produce no effect on the experimental group relative to the control group.

(48) *obsession.* See *(10).*

(49) *operant conditioning.* See *(9).*

(50) *parameter, statistic.* A parameter is a constant value that describes a characteristic of a population. A statistic is a variable value that describes a characteristic of a sample from a population.

(a) A psychologist tested the IQs of all 25 students in Miss Blakeley's 1977 fourth grade class. He found that the mean IQ was 105. If this class were the population of interest,

then the mean of 105 would be a population parameter. (See item *53* for the definition of *population*.)

(b) If, in the above example, Miss Blakeley's 1977 fourth grade class were viewed as a sample of fourth grade classes throughout the United States, then the mean of 105 would be a sample statistic. (See item *53* for the definition of *sample*.)

(51) *performance.* See *(38)*.

(52) *phenotype.* See *(27)*.

(53) *population, sample.* A population is the universe of cases to which an investigator wants to generalize his or her results. A sample is a subset of a population.

(a) If an investigator views Miss Blakeley's 1977 fourth grade class as a population, then any generalizations he or she makes from data obtained from the class will be limited to that class only.

(b) If an investigator views Miss Blakeley's 1977 fourth grade class as a sample, then generalizations he or she makes from data obtained from the class will be to the population of which Miss Blakeley's class is a subset. The more diverse the population, the less likely is Miss Blakeley's class to be representative of the population, and thus, the less likely are the data to be generalizable. One could have more confidence in generalizations to the entire fourth grade at Miss Blakeley's school than in generalizations to the fourth grades of the entire United States.

(54) *primacy, recency.* Primacy effects are effects that occur at the beginning of some temporal sequence. Recency effects are effects that occur at the end of some temporal sequence.

(a) The primacy effect in free recall is the tendency for people to remember items from the beginning of a list better than they remember items from the middle of a list.

(b) The recency effect in free recall is the tendency for people to remember items from the end of a list better than they remember items from the middle of a list.

(55) *ratio IQ*.   See *(18)*.

(56) *recency*.   See *(54)*.

(57) *regression*.   See *(26)*.

(58) *reliability, validity*.   Reliability refers to how well or consistently a test measures whatever the test measures. Validity refers to how well a test measures what it is supposed to measure. Thus, a perfectly reliable test can be completely invalid if it measures something well but not what it is intended to measure. A perfectly valid test, however, must be perfectly reliable, since if the test measures what it is supposed to measure perfectly, it must measure what it does in fact measure perfectly.

(a) The test of finger tapping speed proved to be highly reliable, providing consistent estimates of people's finger tapping abilities. The test of intelligence proved to be only moderately reliable, providing only somewhat consistent estimates of people's measured intelligence.

(b) The highly reliable test of finger tapping speed proved to be invalid as a predictor of school achievement. The moderately reliable intelligence test proved to be moderately valid as a predictor of school achievement. In this case, the more reliable test was less valid for a specific purpose to which it was poorly suited. Although reliability places an upper bound on validity, it is no guarantee of validity.

(59) *repression, suppression*.   Repression is a defense mechanism whereby a thought or feeling is removed from consciousness. Suppression is a defense mechanism whereby a thought or feeling remains in consciousness, but is not overtly expressed. People are aware of suppressed, but not repressed material.

(a) The patient had long ago repressed all memories of his brutal grandfather. At the therapy sessions, he honestly denied ever even having known his grandfather.

(b) The psychologist's therapy sessions with the student were getting nowhere, because the student suppressed any information that he thought might embarrass him in the psychologist's eyes.

(60) *significant.* A statistically significant result is one that enables an investigator to reject a null hypothesis (see item *47*). Statistical significance is sometimes contrasted to practical significance. A result can be statistically significant but not practically significant. Whenever the term *significant* is used by itself, it should be used only to refer to the technical meaning of *statistical significance.* Do not use the word to refer to any result that you think is important.

(a) The large difference between means in the two groups was statistically significant, enabling the psychologist to reject the null hypothesis of no difference between the groups.

(61) *simulation.* See *(5).*

(62) *state, trait.* A state is a temporary mood or frame of mind. A trait is a permanent disposition.

(a) Anxiety as a state refers to a temporary frame of mind in which the individual feels uneasy or apprehensive for no clear reason.

(b) Anxiety as a trait refers to a permanent disposition of an individual to feel uneasy or apprehensive for no clear reason.

(63) *subconscious, unconscious.* The subconscious (or preconscious) contains cognitions that are not conscious, but can be brought into consciousness with little or no effort. The unconscious contains cognitions and feelings of which we are unaware, and that can be brought into consciousness only with difficulty.

(a) As he completed the first sentence of his paper, the ideas for his second sentence glided from his subconscious to his conscious thoughts.

(b) The girl's desire to excel over her three sisters was unconscious, and showed itself only in her behavior and in her repeated dreams of athletic conquests over three familiar but not quite recognizable opponents.

(64) *suppression.*   See *(59)*.

(65) *trait.*   See *(62)*.

(66) *unconscious.*   See *(63)*.

(67) *validity.*   See *(58)*.

(68) *variability, variance.*   The variability of a set of observations refers to the amount of dispersion or spread in the observations. The variance of a set of observations refers to a specific measure of the amount of dispersion: $\Sigma(x^2) / N$, where x is the deviation of each score from the mean and N the number of cases. The term *variance* should be used only to refer to this specific measure, not to refer loosely to the amount of dispersion in the observations.

(a) The scores in the sample showed very little variability.

(b) The variance of the scores in the sample was only 4 points.

(69) *variance.*   See *(68)*.

(70) *white noise.*   White noise is noise composed of sounds of all frequencies. It is called white noise as an analogy to white color, which is composed of colors of all wavelengths. It otherwise has no relation to white or any other color.

(a) White noise was piped into the testing room in order to distract subjects from the difficult memory task.

CHAPTER 6

American Psychological Association Guidelines for Psychology Papers

This chapter summarizes the guidelines for preparing a psychology paper presented in the *Publication Manual of the American Psychological Association,* Second Edition (1974). This manual should be consulted for a complete list of guidelines. If you intend to submit a paper for publication, then you cannot afford to be without this manual. It can be obtained from Publication Sales, American Psychological Association, 1200 Seventeenth Street, N. W., Washington, D. C. 20036.

All examples used to illustrate principles in this chapter are fictitious.

Typing the Paper

RULES OF FORMAT

Paper. Type your paper on one side only of heavy, white, $8\frac{1}{2} \times 11$ inch paper. Do not use onionskin, which lacks durability, or erasable paper, which smudges easily. Do not paste or glue together pieces of pages. Retype those pages that otherwise would require pasting.

Margins. Set your margins to leave 1 to 1½ inches at the top, bottom, and both sides of each page. Allow for a six-inch line. This length is obtained by allowing 60 characters of pica (large) typeface, or 72 characters of elite (small) typeface.

Vertical spacing. Double space between all lines, without exception. There may be times when you are tempted to single space—in writing references, footnotes, block quotations, tables, and the like. Do not succumb to the temptation. Your paper should be double spaced throughout.

Horizontal spacing. Begin each new paragraph by indenting five spaces; type all other lines starting from a uniform left margin. Leave *(a)* no space after internal periods in abbreviations (e.g., U.S.A., U.K.), *(b)* one space after commas and semicolons, *(c)* one space after internal periods in first and middle initials (e.g., H. B. Hinkelmeyer), *(d)* two spaces after colons, except in ratios, where there are no spaces, and *(e)* two spaces after periods ending sentences.

Numbering pages. Number pages consecutively, starting with the abstract. Use arabic numerals. The only pages after the abstract that are not numbered are the figures. Number pages in the upper right hand corner. Above each page number, write the first few words of the title, so that if pages become separated from the manuscript, they can be returned to it later.

RULES OF LEGIBILITY

Typewriter ribbon. Use a fresh, black typewriter ribbon. Old typewriter ribbons often produce faint copy, which is difficult and unpleasant to read. Colored typewriter ribbons (e.g., red, green, blue) produce copy that does not reproduce well, and in almost every case, the color is lost in the reproduction process.

Erasures. Erasure is best produced by correction fluid, paper, or tape. Do not strike over letters, type insert pages (e.g., page 15a to be inserted in the middle of or after page 15), or write in the margins. If there are large numbers of corrections on a page, retype the page.

Additions. If lengthy additions are required on a page, the page should be retyped. If a brief addition is required, it can be typed or printed in pencil above the word or line to be corrected. Insert a caret ($\wedge$) in the appropriate place.

Grammar

PUNCTUATION

Comma.　A comma should be used

(1) before *and* and *or* in a series of three or more items.

The subject, confederate, and experimenter all entered the room together.

(2) before and after a nonrestrictive clause (i.e., a clause that is non-essential to the sentence).

An empty box, which had been rigged to look like a lie detector, was placed on a table next to the subject.

(3) to separate two coordinate clauses joined by a conjunction.

The experimenter pretended to activate the lie detector, and the confederate disappeared into an adjoining room with a one-way mirror.

A comma should not be used

(1) before or after a restrictive clause (i.e., a clause that limits or further defines the word it modifies).

The button that the experimenter pushed served only to impress the subject.

(2) between two parts of a compound predicate.

> The experimenter attached two fake electrodes to the subject's wrists and told the subject that the truth or falsity of each response would be recorded by the machine.

(3) to separate two independent clauses not joined by a conjunction.

> First the subject was asked to answer each question; then he was told that he would receive double pay at the end of the experiment if he succeeded in fooling the "lie detector."

Semicolon. A semicolon should be used to

(1) separate two independent clauses that are not joined by a conjunction.

> The experimenter then proceeded to ask the subject a series of embarrassing questions; he pretended to be surprised at the subject's responses.

(2) separate items that already contain commas.

> The sets of questions asked by the experimenter dealt with sex, swearing, bathroom habits; masculinity, undressing habits, thumbsucking; or private fantasies, nightmares, academic failures.

Colon. A colon should be used

(1) before a final phrase or clause that amplifies the material that comes before it.

> Most subjects initially hesitated to answer the questions: They stared at the experimenter in disbelief.

(2) in ratios and proportions.

> The proportions of subjects answering the questions honestly were 15:25, 13:37, and 18:26 in the

three groups receiving the different sets of questions.

Hyphen. A hyphen should be used in

(1) a compound with a participle if the compound precedes a noun it modifies.

The truth-telling subjects showed less fidgeting than the lie-telling ones.

(2) a phrase used as an adjective if the phrase precedes a noun it modifies.

A subject-by-subject analysis of the results showed strong differences in the honesty with which various individuals answered the questions.

(3) an adjective-noun compound that precedes and modifies another noun.

High-anxiety subjects were less honest in their answers than were low-anxiety subjects.

(4) all compounds involving *self*.

Self-report data indicated that high-anxiety subjects were more worried than low-anxiety subjects that honest answers would later be used against them.

(5) all compounds involving a number as the first element in which the compound precedes a noun.

Second-session results showed the same trends, although in this session the trends failed to reach significance.

A hyphen should not be used in

(1) a compound with an adverb ending in *-ly*.

A widely expressed fear was that the subjects' responses would not really be kept confidential.

(2) a compound involving a comparative or superlative.

> A less common fear was that the experimenter would know from the "lie detector" which responses were truthful and which were not.

(3) a modifier with a letter or numeral as the second term.

> The Session 2 data seem to have been affected less by these fears than the Session 1 data.

Dash. A dash should be used to indicate an interruption in the continuity or flow of a sentence.

> The subjects who lied in answering every question—all of them members of the high-anxiety group—confessed that they thought the "lie detector" was nothing more than an empty box.

Double quotation marks. Double quotation marks should be used

(1) to introduce a word or phrase used in a special or unusual way; use quotation marks only the first time the word is used.

> The experimenter divided the subjects into two groups: the "con artists" and the "apple polishers."

(2) to reproduce material that is quoted verbatim.

> The con artists had taken to heart the experimental instruction that "you should lie whenever you think you can get away with it." The apple polishers seemed to have ignored or disbelieved this instruction, and almost always told the truth.

(3) for names of articles.

> The experimenter planned to name his article, "An Experimental Investigation of Con Artistry."

Quotation marks should not be used

(1) to qualify statements or to hedge bets.

> The apple polishers were relieved when the experiment was over; the con artists begged for more (not "begged" for more).

(2) for long quotations; use block format.

> The experimenter debriefed the subjects at the end of the experiment:

>> The purpose of this experiment was to provide a source of examples for *Writing the Psychology Paper.* The experiment itself made no sense and had no purpose other than to provide the examples. I hope you enjoyed this meaningful activity.

Observe the following rules in using quotation marks:

(1) Omission of material within a sentence of a quotation is indicated by the use of three ellipsis points (. . .). Omission of material between sentences of a quotation is indicated by four ellipsis points (. . . .). Ellipsis points should not be used at the beginning or end of a quotation.

> According to McGoof (1974), "The difference between groups . . . was statistically but not practically significant" (p. 303).

> As he left the room, the subject said to the experimenter, "I hope I wasn't really supposed to write down the words in the order in which they were read. . . . I know the instructions said to, but I didn't see the point."

(2) Insertion of material within a sentence of a quotation is indicated by brackets. Such insertions are usually used to clarify the quotation for the reader, or to make the grammar of

the quotation consistent with the sentence or paragraph in which it is embedded.

> According to the instructions, "This test [should be] timed for 30 minutes."

(3) Two kinds of changes are permissible in quotations without any indication to the reader: *(a)* The first letter of the first quoted word may be changed from a capital to a small letter, or vice versa; and *(b)* the punctuation mark at the end of the quotation may be changed to fit the syntax of the sentence in which you have embedded the quotation. All other changes must be indicated by ellipsis or brackets.

> The sentence, "He ate the cheese," may be cited as, "He ate the cheese."

(4) The source of a direct quotation should always be cited. Include in the citation the author(s), year, and page number(s) of the quotation. If the quotation is *(a)* in the middle of a sentence, cite the source of the quotation in parentheses immediately proceeding the quotation; *(b)* at the end of a sentence, cite the page number in parentheses after the end of the quotation, but before the final punctuation mark; *(c)* in block format, cite the page number in parentheses after the end of the quotation and after the final punctuation mark.

> According to the author, "None of the mice ate the cheese until they had finished the task" (Rattan, 1976, p. 108), so they were hungry.
>
> Rattan (1976) found that "none of the mice ate the cheese until they had finished the task" (p. 108).
>
> According to Rattan (1976),
>
> > None of the mice ate the cheese until they had finished the task. After they ate the cheese, six mice proceeded to redo the task, while the other nine mice marched back to their cages. (p. 108)

(5) Long quotations may require permission from the owner of the copyright on the material. APA policy permits use of up to 500 words without permission. Copyright owners vary in the number of words permitted, however, and so for quotations of 100 or more words it is wise to check the policy of the copyright owner. Even if the copyright owner is a journal or book company, it is a common courtesy to request permission from the author as well as the company. If multiple authors are involved, request permission only of the senior author.

Single quotation marks.   Single quotation marks should be used for quotations within quotations.

> The experimenter, as if to emphasize the pointlessness of the experiment, said to the subjects, "Remember the well known proverb: 'All's well that ends well.'"

Parentheses.   Parentheses should be used to

(1) set off items that are structurally independent from the rest of the sentence.

> After debriefing, subjects were given a questionnaire in which they were asked their reactions to the experiment (see Table 1).

(2) enclose the date of references cited within the text.

> The questionnaire was adopted with minor modifications from one used by Bozo (1971).

(3) enclose abbreviations for previously cited items.

> Subjects were also given the Toliver Test of Tolerance for Trauma (TTTT).

(4) enclose letters or numbers enumerating items in a series.

Finally, subjects were given three ability tests: *(a)* the Penultimate Test of Pencil-Pushing Power, *(b)* the Scofield Scale of Hand-Foot Coordination, and *(c)* the Williams Test of Will Power.

(5) enclose the page number of a cited quotation.

The Williams test seemed particularly appropriate for this experiment, since it is described in the manual as "an invalid test of practically anything an investigator might want to measure" (p. 26).

(6) group terms in mathematical expressions.

On the Williams test, there is a correction for guessing, so that overall score is a function of both right and wrong answers:

$R - (W / 4)$.

(7) enclose enumeration of equations.

The overall score on the Williams test can be converted to a standard score

$$z = (X - \bar{X}) / SD. \tag{1}$$

In this notation, z is the standard score, X the overall score, $\bar{X}$ the mean of the scores, and SD the standard deviation of the scores.

Brackets.　Brackets should be used to

(1) enclose material inserted in a quotation by someone other than the quoted writer or speaker.

A subject remarked as he left the experiment, "This is the most pointless [experiment] I've ever been in."

(2) enclose parenthetical material within parentheses.

(The confederate [see *Method* section] was inclined to agree.)

CAPITALIZATION

When to use capitals. A capital letter should be used for the first letters of

(1) nouns followed by numerals or letters indicating membership in an enumerated series (except for enumeration of pages, chapters, rows, and columns).

> In Session 1 of a new experiment on pencil pushing, subjects were asked to copy on page 1 of their booklets a paragraph of printed material.

(2) trade and brand names.

> Subjects used a Pengo Permapencil to do their copying.

(3) exact, complete titles of tests.

> Three tests of pencil pushing were administered: *(a)* the Penultimate Test of Pencil-Pushing Power, *(b)* the Staley Push-a-Pencil Test, and *(c)* the Pennsylvania Pencil Inventory.

(4) names of factors from a factor analysis.

> A factor analysis of the tests revealed just one reliable factor, which the experimenter called Pencil-Pushing Speed.

(5) names of university departments referring to specific departments within specific universities.

> The experiment was conducted under the auspices of the Department of Psychology, Zingo University.

(6) major words in titles of books and journal articles mentioned in the text of a psychology paper.

> The article reporting the experiment was to be entitled, "A Factor Analysis of Pencil-Pushing Power."

(7) the first word in titles of books and articles cited in the references of a psychology paper.

> Muddlehead, M. M. A factor analysis of pencil-pushing power. *Journal of Junky Experiments,* 1976, *5,* 406–409.

(8) all major words of journal names appearing in the references of a psychology paper.

> (see above example)

(9) major words of table titles.

> Table 1
>
> Loadings of Ability Tests on Pencil-Pushing Speed Factor

(10) first words of figure captions.

> Figure 1. A typical sample of copied material.

When not to use capitals. A capital letter should not be used for first letters of

(1) names of conditions or groups in an experiment.

> Subjects in the experiment were divided into two groups, fast pencil pushers and slow pencil pushers.

(2) names of effects taken from analyses of variance.

> An analysis of variance revealed no difference in school achievement as a function of pencil-pushing speed.

(3) shortened or inexact titles of tests or titles of unpublished tests.

> Scores on the Staley test showed no practice effect.

(4) nouns preceding a variable.

> Scores in session n were no higher on the average than were scores in session n-1.

(5) names of laws, theories, and hypotheses.

> The experimenter used a unifactor theory of pencil pushing to explain his results.

ITALICS

When to use italics.   Italics are indicated in manuscripts by underlining the words or symbols to be italicized. Italics should be used for

(1) titles of books, periodicals, and microfilms.

> The article relating bumps on the head to claustrophobia was published in the journal, *Phrenology Today*.

> The author didn't think a book entitled *Bump It or Lump It* would sell enough copies to make writing the book worthwhile.

(2) introducing new, technical, or important terms.

> All subjects in the experiment were told the meaning of the word, *phrenology*.

(3) letters, words, phrases, or sentences cited as linguistic examples.

> Some subjects did not even realize that *phrenology* was a noun.

(4) letters used as statistical symbols or algebraic variables.

> The difference in number of bumps on the head between claustrophobic and nonclaustrophobic subjects was not significant, $t(32) = 0.26, p > .05$.

> The phrenologist still argued that the relation between degree of claustrophobia (y) and number of bumps on the head (x) could be expressed by the equation, $y = 7x + 2$.

(5) volume numbers in reference lists.

> Bumpo, B. P. The relation between bumps on the head and claustrophobia. *Phrenology Today*, 1921, *13,* 402–406.

When not to use italics.   Italics should not be used for

(1) common foreign words and abbreviations.

> The a priori likelihood of a relation between number of bumps on the head and degree of claustrophobia seemed remote.

> The remarks of Zootz et al. (1949) vis-a-vis errors in counting numbers of bumps are still relevant today.

(2) names of Greek letters.

> Zootz and his colleagues noted that there are two kinds of bumps, alpha (α) bumps and beta (β) bumps, and that only alpha bumps should be counted.

(3) emphasis unless the emphasis would be lost without italics.

> Zootz and his colleagues emphasized that there was no known relation between number of beta bumps and claustrophobia.

(4) abbreviations.

> The National Phrenological Society (NPS) dissociated itself from the work of both Bumpo and Zootz.

SPELLING

The standard reference used by American Psychological Association journals for spelling is *Webster's New Collegiate Dictionary* (1973). *Webster's Third New International Dictionary* (1971) should be consulted for spellings of words not in the collegiate volume. In cases where two or more spellings are acceptable, use the first, preferred spelling.

ABBREVIATIONS

When to use abbreviations. Use abbreviations sparingly. Explain each abbreviation the first time it is used, except in the case of *(1)* below. Abbreviations may be used

(1) without explanation if they are listed as word entries (i.e., are not labeled *abbr*) in *Webster's New Collegiate Dictionary* (1973).

> The subject scored 108 on the IQ test.

(2) even if they are not in the dictionary but are frequently used in a relevant journal.

> The subject's average response time (RT) in responding to test items was 6.52 sec.

(3) for standard Latin terms, statistics, and reference terms.

> Blimpey et al. (1966) had full confidence in the IQ test they used.

(4) for metric units.

> To give readers an idea of the length of the test, the authors noted that the test booklet was two cm thick.

When to use periods in abbreviations. Periods should be used with

(1) initials of names.

> A. C. Acney discovered the little known Acney effect.

(2) abbreviations of state and territory names.

> He discovered the effect in his little lab in Washington, D. C.

(3) Latin abbreviations.

The discovery was made at exactly 8:00 a.m.

(4) reference abbreviations.

The effect is described in Vol. 3 of the *Autobiography of A. C. Acney*.

(5) nonmetric measurement abbreviations.

This lengthy book weighs three lb., and can be used to press leaves.

When not to use periods in abbreviations. Periods should not be used with

(1) capital letter abbreviations, including acronyms.

The now discredited Acney effect relates IQ to facial complexion. Acney was unsuccessful in getting the report of his findings into any APA journal.

(2) abbreviations of metric units.

Expressed in metric units, the weight of Vol. 3 of Acney's autobiography is 6.6 kg, 6.6 kg more than the book is worth.

When not to use abbreviations. Do not use nonstandard abbreviations or abbreviations that you make up. Do not use the abbreviations *S* for subject, *E* for experimenter, or *O* for observer. Although these abbreviations were once standard, they are no longer used.

Headings

APA editorial guidelines make provision for four levels of headings:

(1) a centered heading typed all in capitals.

(2) an italicized center heading with main words capitalized.

(3) a heading flush with the left margin, with major words capitalized.

(4) an indented paragraph heading with the first word capitalized and the last word followed by a period.

The complete set of four headings is usually needed only in very long articles, for example, reports of multiple experiments. The rules for headings are these:

Rule #1: If you use only one level of heading, as in short articles, use the second (2) level described above.

Rule #2: If you use two levels of headings, as in articles of average length, use the second (2) and third (3) levels described above.

Rule #3: If you use three levels of headings, as in longer articles, use the second (2), third (3), and fourth (4) levels described above.

Rule #4: If you use four levels of headings, as in long articles and monographs, use all four levels of headings described above.

This book does not follow this sequence of headings.

An example using all four levels of headings is the following:

EXPERIMENT I
Method
Design
Independent variables.

Quantitative Issues

UNITS OF MEASUREMENT

The American Psychological Association has adopted the metric system in all APA journals, and other journals have generally followed suit. Authors therefore should express measurements in metric units wherever possible. If measurements are expressed in other kinds of units, metric equivalents should be given.

STATISTICS

Statistics can be presented in the text, in tables, or in figures. The author of a paper must choose the means that most effectively communicates his data. Frequently used statistics (e.g., the mean, t, F) can be used without explanation. Infrequently used statistics (e.g., c_p) should be explained, and a reference for the statistic cited. A reference should also be given for use of a statistic in a controversial way (e.g., the F statistic when sample variances are widely discrepant).

The standard format for presentation of inferential statistics in text calls for inclusion of the name of the statistic, the degrees of freedom for the statistic (if relevant), the value of the statistic, and the probability level associated with the statistic. This information is presented in the following way:

> Subjects informed of the relation between lists recalled significantly more words than subjects not informed of this relation, $t(68) = 2.93, p < .01$.

> The personality scale did not differentiate among compulsive, hysterical, and normal subjects, $F(2, 28) = 1.18, p > .05$.

Note that the use of the less-than sign ($<$) indicates a significant difference, but the use of the greater-than sign ($>$) indicates a nonsignificant difference.

EQUATIONS

General principles. Several general principles apply to the presentation of equations:

(1) Space mathematical expressions as you would space

words, keeping in mind that the primary consideration is legibility.

$$y = a / (b + c)$$

(2) Align mathematical expressions carefully. Subscripts generally precede superscripts, but primes occur immediately following the primed letter or symbol.

$$y = x_p{}^3 + x'_q{}^2$$

(3) Punctuate all equations, however presented, as you would any expression, mathematical or not.

> The standard formula was used for computing IQ: $IQ = MA / CA$.

(4) Parentheses ( ), brackets [ ], and braces { } should be used in that order to avoid ambiguity.

$$y = a / (b + c)$$
$$y = a / [(b + c) \cdot (d - e)]$$
$$y = \{a / [(b + c) \cdot (d - e)]\} + f$$

(5) Use the percentage symbol (%) only when it is preceded by a number. Otherwise, use the word *percentage*.

> Only 18% of the sample responded to the questionnaire.

> The percentage of respondents was disappointing.

Equations merged with text. Short and simple equations that will not have to be referred to later in the text can be placed in the midst of a line of text. Follow these rules:

(1) Fractions presented in the midst of a line of text should be indicated by use of a slash.

> The data indicated that for any values of a and b, $y = a / b$.

(2) The equation should not project above or below the line. If it does, use the format for equations described below.

Equations separated from text. Equations should be separated from the text if *(a)* they are referred to later, *(b)* they are complex, or *(c)* they project above or below a single line of text. Equations separated from the text should be numbered consecutively, with the number enclosed in parentheses and near the right margin of the page.

$$RT = 5x^2 + \frac{y + 8}{2n} + \frac{z^3 + 5}{1/n} \tag{1}$$

NUMBERS

General principles. Several general principles apply to the use of numbers in text:

(1) Rules for cardinal numbers (e.g., *two*) and ordinal numbers (e.g., *second*) are the same (see below), except for percentiles and quartiles. Percentiles and quartiles should always be expressed in figures.

> The boy's score placed him in the 5th percentile.

(2) Use arabic rather than roman numerals wherever possible. Use roman numerals, however, where convention calls for their use.

> The probability of a Type I error was less than 5%.

(3) For numbers greater than or equal to 1,000, use commas between every group of three digits.

> His response was timed at 1,185 msec.

(4) In writing decimals, do not place a zero before the decimal point if the number is less than one.

> The proportion of subjects finishing the task was .86.

(5) Use decimal notation instead of mixed fractions

wherever possible. Do not use decimals, though, if their use is awkward.

> The maximum score on the test was 8.5 out of 10.
> The oldest child in the experimental group was $5\frac{1}{2}$ years old.

Numbers expressed in words. Numbers should be expressed in words if

(1) they are between zero and nine inclusive (with exceptions described in the next section).

> There were only six children in the sample.

(2) they begin a sentence, regardless of whether or not they are less than 10.

> Six children were tested.

Numbers expressed in figures. Numbers should be expressed in figures if they satisfy any of the following conditions. Notice that all conditions except the first are exceptions to rule *(1)* above for expressing numbers in words. Express numbers in figures if they are

(1) greater than or equal to 10.

> There were 18 adults in the sample.

(2) ages.

> All of the adults were over 21 years of age.

(3) times and dates.

> The experiment took place between the hours of 8 a.m. and 10 a.m. on April 6, 1976.

(4) percentages.

> Over 90% of the subjects finished the task.

(5) ratios.

> This was a ratio of 9:1.

(6) fractions or decimals.

> The corresponding fraction was 9/10, and the corresponding decimal .9.

(7) exact sums of money.

> Subjects were each paid $3 for participation in the experiment.

(8) scores and points on scales.

> The student received a score of 8.32 on a scale ranging from 0 to 9.

(9) references to numerals as numerals.

> The numeral 0 was placed next to each true item; the numeral 1 was placed next to each false item.

(10) page numbers.

> The students were told to write their identification numbers on page 1.

(11) series of four or more items.

> Students were assigned consecutive identification numbers: The first four students, for example, were assigned the numbers 1, 2, 3, and 4 respectively.

(12) numbers grouped for comparison either between or within sentences if any of the numbers is 10 or greater.

> There were 11 subjects in the first group, but only 9 subjects in the second group.

SERIATION

Within a paragraph.   Seriation within a paragraph is indicated by lowercase letters written in parentheses. Do not italicize the letters.

> The five categories of words to be recalled were *(a)* fruits, *(b)* animals, *(c)* nuts, *(d)* countries, and *(e)* oceans.

Of paragraphs. Seriation of paragraphs is indicated by arabic numerals followed by periods. Do not enclose the numbers in parentheses.

> The experimenter used a three-step procedure:
>
> 1. The experimenter greeted the subject as the subject entered the room.
>
> 2. A confederate entered the room and asked for the time of day. He appeared to be in a state of great confusion.
>
> 3. The confederate noticed the subject, and struck up a conversation with him.

(Note that neither of these seriation conventions has been followed in the present book.)

References

CITATIONS IN TEXT

Standard formats. References that are generally available may be cited either directly or indirectly:

(1) If the author is cited directly, the date proceeds the author citation in parentheses.

> Nimbus (1962) found that cloud formations can be used to predict persons' moods.

(2) If the author is cited indirectly, both the author's name and the date are placed in parentheses.

> It has been found that cloud formations can be used to predict persons' moods (Nimbus, 1962).
>
> This result has since been replicated (Nimbus, 1963; Stratus, 1964).

(3) If the date is mentioned in the text, it need not be repeated in parentheses.

> In 1962, Nimbus found that cloud formations can be used to predict persons' moods.

(4) If a work is cited more than once on the same page or within a few pages, the date need not be repeated if there is no resulting ambiguity.

> Nimbus's (1962) work on cloud formations and mood has received little attention. The lack of attention may be due to Nimbus's opening sentence: "Only a fool would take the work reported here seriously" (p. 1).

(5) Multiple references to work of the same author published in the same year are assigned lowercase letters to distinguish them when they are cited. The letters should be assigned alphabetically by title name.

> Snow (1964a) has concluded that precipitation can dampen people's spirits. Snow (1964b) has argued that frozen precipitation is most demoralizing.

Multiple authors. Follow these rules in citing work of multiple authors:

(1) If a work has just two authors, cite both names and the date every time you make a citation.

> McLeod and O'Dowd (1962) found an artifact in Nimbus's (1962) study.   (First citation)
>
> McLeod and O'Dowd (1962) corrected the artifact.   (Later citation)

(2) If a work has more than two authors, cite all names and the date the first time you make the citation; in later citations, you need only cite the first author, followed by "et al." and the date. If two different pieces of work shorten to the same form, then always cite the full references to avoid confusion.

> McLeod, O'Dowd, and Giroud (1967) found no relation between cloud formations and mood.
>   (First citation)

> McLeod et al. (1967) did not investigate cloud formations during tornados or hurricanes, however. (Later citations)

(3) If citations with multiple authors are made directly, the names of the authors are connected by "and." If citations are made indirectly, the names of the authors are connected by "&":

> McLeod and O'Dowd (1962) found the artifact.
>
> An artifact was discovered (McLeod & O'Dowd, 1962).

No author. If you cite a reference with no author, use the first two or three words of the entry as described in the references. In this case, the entry will usually be cited by title.

> The pamphlet suggests ways of improving one's memory ("Tips on Memory," 1931).

Corporate author. A corporate author may be cited instead of a personal one. Lengthy corporate names should be abbreviated only if they are readily identifiable in the reference list.

> The book presented 15 ways to make friends (Golden Friendship Society, 1968).

Authors with the same surname. If you refer to more than one author with the same surname, include each author's initials each time you cite the author.

> S. Jones (1973) disagreed with the interpretations drawn by E. Jones (1970).

THE REFERENCE LIST

The References section of a paper contains an alphabetical list of the generally available references cited in the text of the paper. References to more than one work of the same author are arranged by order of date of publication, with earlier works listed first. Each reference should include the author(s), title, and facts of publication. Details regarding format are given in Chapter 2: The format for the references is the same as the format for the author cards described in that chapter. Here are some examples of different kinds of references:

References

Balderdash, H. Q. *Writing for meaning*. Los Angeles: Perfection Press, 1969

Crumpet, C. D., & Donut, D. C. *Sugar tastes good and is good for you* (Vol. 1). Honolulu: Sugar Promotion Press, 1975.

Finn, D., Jr. Breathing in fish. In G. Trout & H. Bass (Eds.), *The physiology of fish*. Nantucket, Mass.: Fisherman's Press, 1970.

Firestone, N. Z. You can prevent pyromania. *Journal of Exotic Ailments,* 1974, *15*, 63-68.

Gamboling for fun and profit. Las Vegas: American Exercise Institute, 1958.

Lemon, B. J. *Vitamin C in your diet* (2nd ed.). Miami: Citrus Press, 1974.

Lohne, E. Z., & Sharke, P. P. Should usery be a crime? *Money Minder's Digest*, in press.

Pompus, V. Q. (Ed.), *Encyclopedia of knowledge* (16 vols.). San Francisco: Worldwide, 1970.

Reference Notes

CITATIONS IN TEXT

Some references are not widely available, and are not listed as ordinary references. Examples of hard-to-get references are unpublished manuscripts not yet in press, technical reports, research reports distributed by their source on a limited basis, papers presented at meetings, proceedings of symposia, and personal communications. Such references are listed as reference notes. Reference notes are cited differently from standard references. If cited directly, the name of the source appears and is followed by a note number in parentheses. If cited indirectly, the name and subsequent note number both appear in parentheses.

> Dunse (Note 1) has claimed that he can raise anyone's IQ score significantly.
>
> One method of raising IQ scores is to give test takers the answer key (Dunse, Note 1).

When both standard references and reference notes appear together in a list, the reference notes should follow the references.

> Other methods of raising IQ scores have also been proposed (Abel, 1966; Baker, 1968; Cain, 1973; Bunker, Note 2).

THE REFERENCE NOTES LIST

The format of reference notes is similar to that of references. The reference notes are presented separately from the references, immediately preceding them. (See Chapter 3 for the ordering of parts of a manuscript.) Here are some examples of reference notes:

Reference Notes

1. Dunse, J. C. *How to raise your IQ score.* Unpublished manuscript, 1968. Available from the Center for Mind Expansion, 1000 Utopia Lane, Paragon, New Hampshire.
2. Bunker, B. B. *What IQ tests really measure.* Book in preparation, 1976.

3. Veritas, A. K. *Cheating is its own punishment: A reply to Dunse*. Paper presented at the meeting of the Clean-Living Society, Seattle, 1973.
4. Lux, C. T. Personal communication, October 6, 1975.
5. Wall, K. L. *Good fences make bad neighbors* (Tech. Rep. 013). New York: Honcho University, Department of Psychology, 1971.

Footnotes

KINDS OF FOOTNOTES

Acknowledgement and author identification. This kind of footnote *(a)* acknowledges the basis of a study, *(b)* acknowledges financial support for a study, *(c)* acknowledges assistance in preparing, conducting, analyzing, or reporting a study, *(d)* elaborates upon or notes a change of an author's affiliation, or *(e)* provides an address to which requests for reprints can be sent. Combinations of these four functions may be combined in a single footnote. The example below combines all these functions.

> This study is based upon a doctoral dissertation submitted in partial fulfillment of the requirements for the Ph.D. degree at Prestige University. The research was supported by grant G107H5 to the author from the National Institute of Rodent Research. I thank Whyte Meise for assistance in conducting the study. The author is now at Rocky Ridge State College. Requests for reprints should be sent to Phineas Phlom, Department of Psychology, Rocky Ridge State College, Small Town, Vermont.

Content footnotes. Content footnotes are used for material that elaborates upon the text, but is not directly relevant to it.

Since these footnotes can distract the reader, they should be used sparingly. Before using such a footnote, you should decide whether the material might be better incorporated into the text or deleted.

[1]The only ill effect upon the subject resulting from the treatment was a deep fear of furry animals, a fear we hope eventually to eradicate.

Reference footnotes. Reference footnotes are used only rarely in psychological reporting. Almost all citations should be made through either references or reference notes. Reference footnotes may be used, however, for legal citations and copyright permissions.

[1]Copyright 1971 by Peanut Press, Inc. Quoted by permission.

Table footnotes. Table footnotes amplify information contained in tables. They are discussed in the section on *Tables*.

NUMBERING OF FOOTNOTES

Footnotes of acknowledgement and author identification do not receive numbers. Content and reference footnotes are numbered consecutively throughout a paper. Footnotes are indicated by arabic numeral superscripts. If a footnote is referred to more than once, subsequent references should use a parenthetical statement rather than a superscript. Footnotes to a table should be lettered consecutively within each table.

Jones (1958) found that subjects suffered from few ill aftereffects.[1]

Critics have lambasted Jones's (1958) alleged insensitivity to subjects (see Footnote 1).

PLACEMENT OF FOOTNOTES

In papers to be submitted for publication, footnotes are placed on a separate page after the references (see Chapter 3). In student papers, however, it is often more convenient for the reader if the footnotes are placed at the bottom of the page on which each footnote is cited.

Tables

WHEN TO USE TABLES

Tables enable an author to present large amounts of material concisely. Moreover, they often enable a reader to understand at a glance patterns of data that would be obscure if presented in the text. Tables are expensive for journals to produce, however, so that if you plan to submit a paper for publication, you should present in tabular form only your more important sets of data. Do not duplicate data from one table to another unless it is essential for the comprehension of each table. If duplication seems necessary, you might want first to consider combining the tables in which the duplication occurs. Extensive sets of data should be reported in appendices rather than in the body of the paper.

RELATION BETWEEN TABLES AND TEXT

Three common mistakes in the use of tables are *(a)* duplication in the text of material presented in tables, *(b)* presentation of tables that are unintelligible without reference to the text, and *(c)* presentation of tables with no or minimal discussion. First, data that are presented in tables should be discussed in the text, not re-presented. Guide your reader through the major aspects of each table, but assume that he or she can read the exact values out of each table without your repeating them. Second, construct each table so that your reader is able to understand it without reference to the text. Third, remember that even if the reader is able to understand the table by itself, he or she may not see what conclusions you want to draw. If data are important enough to present in tabular form, they are important enough to discuss.

PARTS OF A TABLE

Table number. Tables should be numbered with arabic numerals in order of appearance. Do not use suffixes to interrelate tables, e.g., Tables 5 and 5A. Tables should have numbers only. Thus, Tables 5 and 5A should be numbered 5 and 6. If you present tables in an appendix, identify them with capital letters, starting with Table A. The table number is written at the top of the table, as shown in Table 1.

Table title. The title of a table should describe concisely what the table is supposed to show. The title should be understandable without reference to the text.

Column headings. Column headings are of four types: stubheads, boxheads, column heads, and spanner heads. The left-hand column of a table is called the stub. The stub usually lists independent variables. The heading for this column is called the *stubhead*. In Table 1, the stubhead is "Analogy Type." The headings at the top of the table are called *boxheads*. A boxhead may cover one or more columns. In Table 1, the boxhead is "Grade," and it covers three columns. When the boxhead covers more than one column, a further subdivision called a *column head* is used. There is just one column head for each column. The column heads in Table 1 are *"n,"* "2," "4," and "6." Occasionally, tables may require headings that cover the entire body of the table. Such headings are called *spanner heads*. In Table 1, there are two spanner heads: "Boys" and

TABLE 1

**Mean Scores of Children at Three Different
Grade Levels on Analogy Tests**

Analogy Type	n	Grade		
		2	4	6
Boys				
Verbal				
Easy	16	14.2	15.1	15.7
Medium	14	9.8	12.6	13.1
Hard	15	4.4	9.5	10.7
Symbolic				
Easy	15	15.5	17.0	17.8
Medium	15	12.6	14.5	15.0
Hard	15	6.0	8.2	9.1
Girls				
Verbal				
Easy	16	15.5	16.8	17.2
Medium	15	11.4	13.6	14.0
Hard	14	7.0	10.4	11.9
Symbolic				
Easy[a]	15	10.4	13.2	15.1
Medium	14	8.5	10.6	12.3
Hard	16	3.9	5.6	7.4

Note. Maximum score = 20.0
[a]One girl did not answer any items, and was therefore removed from the sample.

"Girls." Spanner heads are particularly useful for combining two tables into one. Instead of presenting the data for boys and girls in separate tables, the data are combined into one table.

Notice the simplification that is achieved by the use of a table. The reader looking at Table 1 can see that the complete design of the experiment is two kinds of analogy content by three levels of analogy difficulty by three grade levels by two sexes (2x3x3x2). The design is a complicated one, but can be understood readily by reference to the table.

Body of the table. All numerical values of the same kind in a table should be expressed to the same degree of precision. Use only as much precision as the data justify. Extra digits convey no additional information and clutter the table. Do not include columns of data that can be calculated easily from other columns. For example, if you have two columns entitled "Number Right" and "Number Wrong," and the final score is the difference between these two columns, there is no need to present a third column entitled "Final Score."

Footnotes. Footnotes to a table are of three kinds.

(1) *General notes.* A general note provides further information about the table as a whole. In Table 1, for example, the general note informs the reader of the maximum possible score.

(2) *Specific notes.* A specific note provides further information about one or more entries in the table. Such notes are indicated by letter superscripts attached to the appropriate entries. In Table 1, there is one specific note. If there is more than one note, the notes should be ordered horizontally by rows.

(3) *Probability levels.* Probability levels are used to ascertain the significance of statistical tests. A single asterisk should be used for the highest probability level, and an additional asterisk should be used for each lower probability level.

The number of asterisks used for a given probability level need not be consistent across tables. The most common use of asterisks is for one to represent $p < .05$, two to represent $p < .01$, and three to represent $p < .001$.

When more than one kind of footnote appears in a single table, general footnotes precede specific ones, and specific ones precede probability levels. The footnotes to a single table might look like this:

> *Note.* All subjects were veterans.
>
> [a]Two subjects were caught copying from each other, and were eliminated from this group.
>
> [b]One subject in this group refused to finish the task, and was eliminated.
>
> *$p < .05$
> **$p < .01$
> ***$p < .001$

RULING OF TABLES

Tables may have *(a)* no rules, *(b)* either horizontal or vertical rules, or *(c)* both horizontal and vertical rules. Most journals have standard formats. In deciding which kind of ruling to use (if any), choose the ruling that most facilitates the reader's understanding of the table.

PLACEMENT OF TABLES

In papers submitted for publication, tables are placed after footnotes (see Chapter 3). The following notice should be placed at the point at which the author wants the table inserted:

Insert Table 1 about here

In student papers, tables are often placed at the point in the text at which they are discussed. The reader then does not have to turn to the back of the paper in order to look at the tables.

Figures

WHEN TO USE FIGURES

Figures, like tables, enable an author to present large amounts of information concisely. Their advantage over tables is that they often enable the reader to see at a glance trends that otherwise would not be readily apparent. Figures have the disadvantage, however, that they do not convey precise values of data. For this reason, tables are often preferred.

If you plan to submit an article for publication, you should use figures sparingly, since they are expensive to reproduce. Figures in articles submitted for publication must be of professional quality, and should be submitted as glossy photographs.

Do not duplicate information from one figure to another unless it is essential to comprehension of each figure. If duplication seems necessary, you might want first to consider combining the figures in which the duplication occurs. Presentation of too much data in a single figure, however, gives the figure a cluttered look. Generally, four plots per figure should be the maximum.

RELATION BETWEEN FIGURES AND TEXT

The three common mistakes made in the use of tables apply equally well to figures. First, do not duplicate in the text material that is presented in the figures. Second, do not present figures that are unintelligible without reference to the text. Third, do not present figures without discussion.

CONSTRUCTING FIGURES

Draw figures 8½ x 11 inches or smaller. If you plan to submit your paper for publication, remember that each figure will be reduced in size, so that detail will become harder to see. Draw each figure with black india ink on white drawing paper. If you use graph paper, use only paper with blue ruling, since blue does not reproduce photographically. Lettering should be done with a stencil. Do not use freehand or typescript. In plotting values of a dependent variable against values of an independent variable, place the independent variable on the horizontal axis and the dependent variable on the vertical axis. Each axis should be labeled and the units marked along it. The scale should be chosen so that the plots take up most of the figure. Data points should be indicated by small geometric figures, such as circles, squares, or triangles.

PLACEMENT OF FIGURES

In articles submitted for publication, figures are placed at the end of the article (see Chapter 3). In student papers, however, it is often more convenient to insert the figures at the appropriate place in the text. Similarly, figure captions can be placed directly underneath the figure, rather than in a separate section preceding the figures. If you do place figures at the end, you should use the following notice at each location in which you would want a figure inserted:

Insert Figure 1 about here

FIGURE NUMBERS

Figures are numbered consecutively with arabic numerals, starting with Figure 1. If the article is to be submitted for publication, the figure number should be written on the back, not on the front of the figure.

FIGURE CAPTIONS

A figure caption should describe concisely what the figure is supposed to show. It should be understandable without reference to the text. If you need to add any additional information (as would be supplied in table notes), add it in parentheses after the figure caption.

A Final Word

You should adhere to these rules diligently, whether you submit your paper to a course instructor or to a journal editor. In the former case, your instructor will appreciate your concern for correct format, even if he has not explicitly requested it. In the latter case, a journal editor will expect strict adherence to the rules, and may send back a paper that does not conform to them. A sample student paper typed according to the APA rules is presented in the Appendix.

CHAPTER **7**

References for the Psychology Paper

Authors of psychology papers should be aware of the references available to them. This chapter contains a list of such references. The chapter is divided into two parts. The first part briefly describes general references that may be useful to psychologists in all areas of psychology. The second part of the chapter briefly describes many of the journals psychologists read and consult when writing papers. Wherever possible, descriptions of the journals have been paraphrased from the descriptions provided in the journals themselves. The publisher and address of the publisher are supplied at the end of each description. You should write to this address for further information about the journal and for subscriptions. This address is not appropriate for submission of manuscripts, since manuscripts are submitted to the editor of a journal, not the publisher. Because the editorship of a journal usually changes on a fairly regular basis, the names and addresses of editors are not given in this chapter. They can be obtained by consulting recent issues of each journal. In addition to containing the name and address of the current editor, the inside covers of journals also contain useful information on style, specifications for articles, deviations from APA guidelines, and so on.

General References

BIOGRAPHICAL DIRECTORY OF THE AMERICAN PSYCHOLOGICAL ASSOCIATION

The Biographical Directory of the American Psychological Association lists for each member of the APA his or her name, address, telephone number, education, present major field, areas of specialization, certification as a psychologist, diplomate status, and APA membership status. Also included are a membership roster for each APA division, the APA Bylaws, a list of present and past APA officers, ethical standards, and current data on laws governing the practice of psychology. The Directory, revised every two years, is published by the American Psychological Association, Washington, D.C.

CAREERS IN PSYCHOLOGY

Careers in Psychology describes the variety of careers available in psychology, as well as the salaries they pay and the qualifications required to obtain the jobs. The booklet also includes a general description of the American Psychological Association and its services, a list of related organizations and sources of information, and a bibliography of publications that will be useful to students searching for a career. The booklet, revised in 1975, is published by the American Psychological Association, Washington, D. C.

A COMPREHENSIVE DICTIONARY OF PSYCHOLOGICAL AND PSYCHOANALYTICAL TERMS: A GUIDE TO USAGE

A Comprehensive Dictionary of Psychological and Psychoanalytical Terms: A Guide to Usage contains many of the technical terms most frequently used in psychology and psychoanalysis. The book, published in 1958, is now somewhat out-of-date. The book is by H. B. English and A. C. English, and is published by Langmans, Green, and Company, New York, New York.

DICTIONARY OF BEHAVIORAL SCIENCE

The *Dictionary of Behavioral Science,* published in 1973, defines technical terms in all of the behavioral sciences. It was written by B. B. Wolman, and is published by Van Nostrand-Reinhold Company, New York, New York.

DICTIONARY OF PSYCHOLOGY

The *Dictionary of Psychology*, by J. P. Chaplin, defines technical psychological terms. It also includes appendices containing abbreviations commonly used in psychology, Hull's major symbolic constructs, common Rorschach scoring symbols, Greek letter symbols commonly used in psychology, prefixes, suffixes, and combining forms commonly used in psychological terminology, and commonly used statistical formulas. The book was published in 1968 by the Dell Publishing Company, New York, New York.

ENCYCLOPEDIA OF HUMAN BEHAVIOR

The *Encyclopedia of Human Behavior* contains entries in psychology, psychiatry, and mental health. The two volume set, edited by R. M. Goldenson, was published in 1970 by Doubleday, Garden City, New York.

ENCYCLOPEDIA OF PSYCHOLOGY

The *Encyclopedia of Psychology* is a three-volume work edited by H. J. Eysenck, W. Arnold, and R. Meili. It contains articles of varying lengths by an international team of experts.

For example, the article on abilities was written by H. J. Eysenck, the article on aggression by L. Berkowitz, the article on aphasia by A. R. Luria, and the article on behaviorism by E. R. Hilgard. The encyclopedia was published in 1972 by Herder and Herder, New York, New York.

ETHICAL PRINCIPLES IN THE CONDUCT OF RESEARCH WITH HUMAN PARTICIPANTS

This book contains principles and discussions of issues in research with human participants. Some of the issues dealt with are informed consent, freedom from coercion, anonymity and confidentiality, and use of research results. The book was published in 1973 by the American Psychological Association, Washington, D. C.

GRADUATE STUDY IN PSYCHOLOGY

Graduate Study in Psychology provides information about 500 graduate and postdoctoral programs in the United States and Canada. The book includes information about application procedures, admission requirements, degree requirements, tuition, financial assistance, internships, minority consideration, how to apply for graduate school, stipends available, and day-care facilities. The book is revised annually by the publisher, the American Psychological Association, Washington, D. C.

GUIDE TO REFERENCE BOOKS

The *Guide to Reference Books,* ninth edition, by E. Sheehy, is a standard annotated bibliography for all disciplines. The guide includes both author and subject entries. It functions as a central reference in which most other references are documented. The book was published in 1976 by the American Library Association, Chicago, Illinois.

JOURNAL SUPPLEMENT ABSTRACT SERVICE

The *Journal Supplement Abstract Service* (JSAS) provides access to psychological materials not available through conventional channels. Manuscripts are submitted to the service and reviewed for possible inclusion. If a manuscript is accepted, an abstract of the manuscript appears in the *JSAS Catalog of Selected Documents in Psychology,* which is published quarterly. Accompanying the abstract are the length, price, and ordering information for the document. Documents are reproduced both in standard size and in microfiche format. The service and catalog of documents are provided by the American Psychological Association, Washington, D.C.

NAMES IN THE HISTORY OF PSYCHOLOGY: A BIOGRAPHICAL SOURCEBOOK

Names in the History of Psychology: A Biographical Sourcebook, by L. Zusne, contains brief biographies of many famous psychologists. The book contains pictures of most of the psychologists. The book was published in 1975 by the Hemisphere Publishing Company, Washington, D. C.

PSYCHOLOGICAL ABSTRACTS

Psychological Abstracts is probably the single most valuable general psychological reference. It contains subject and author indices for over 850 journals, technical reports, monographs, and other documents, and it provides a brief, nonevaluative summary of each article. The Abstracts are published monthly by the American Psychological Association, Washington, D.C.

PSYCHOLOGICAL READER'S GUIDE

The *Psychological Reader's Guide* is a bibliographic source reproducing tables of contents from more than 200 journals in psychology. The Guide is published monthly by Elsevier Sequoia S. A., P. O. Box 851, CH 1001 Lausanne 1, Switzerland.

PSYCINFO

PsycINFO is an information retrieval service that provides a computer-assisted search of the *Psychological Abstracts*. Use of the system is described in detail in a *Users Reference Manual* that is updated frequently. The service and manual are supplied by the American Psychological Association, Washington, D. C.

PUBLICATION MANUAL OF THE AMERICAN PSYCHOLOGICAL ASSOCIATION, SECOND EDITION

The *Publication Manual of the American Psychological Association,* Second Edition, is an indispensable guide to the writing of psychology papers for publication. The manual contains chapters on content and organization of a manuscript, writing style, APA editorial style, typing, mailing, proofreading, and the journals of the APA. It also includes a useful bibliography. The manual was published in 1974 by the American Psychological Association, Washington, D. C.

SCIENCE CITATION INDEX

The *Science Citation Index* is an index of who has cited whom in the natural science literature. It includes the fields of natural sciences, medicine, agriculture, technology, and the behavioral sciences. (Because of its inclusion of the behavioral sciences, psychologists will find it largely overlapping with the *Social Science Index* described below.) The index is published quarterly, and is bound into an annual volume. It is published by the Institute for Scientific Information, Philadelphia, Pennsylvania.

SOCIAL SCIENCE CITATION INDEX

The *Social Science Citation Index* is an index of who has cited whom in the social science literature. It is organized both by author and subject cited. Under each author or subject is a list of persons who have made the citation, and the location of the citation. The Index is updated annually and is published by the Institute for Scientific Information, Philadelphia, Pennsylvania.

SOURCES OF INFORMATION IN THE SOCIAL SCIENCES

Sources of Information in the Social Sciences, by C. M. White, is a comprehensive annotated bibliography of references available in the various social sciences. The book contains both author and title indices. It was published in 1964, and hence is somewhat out-of-date. The publisher is Bedminster Press, Totowa, New Jersey.

STANDARDS FOR EDUCATIONAL AND PSYCHOLOGICAL TESTS

Standards for Educational and Psychological Tests establishes guidelines for the development, use, and sale of standardized tests. The standards were revised in 1974 by the American Psychological Association, Washington, D. C.

Journal References

ACTA PSYCHOLOGICA: INTERNATIONAL JOURNAL OF PSYCHONOMICS

Acta Psychologica publishes research in the field of psychonomics, a field defined by the journal as fundamental rather than applied and oriented toward quantitative models rather than verbal theories. Psychonomics is closest to what is usually called experimental psychology, but also overlaps with the fields of biophysics, physiology, neurology, systems analysis, and computer science. The journal is published bimonthly by the North-Holland Publishing Company, P. O. Box 211, Amsterdam, The Netherlands.

AMERICAN BEHAVIORAL SCIENTIST

The *American Behavioral Scientist* publishes general articles in the behavioral sciences. Each issue is devoted to a special topic. Some recent topics have included military ethics and professionalism, social science data archives, social policy research, and age in society. The journal is published bimonthly by Sage Publications, 275 South Beverley Drive, Beverley Hills, California 90212.

AMERICAN JOURNAL OF COMMUNITY PSYCHOLOGY

The *American Journal of Community Psychology* is devoted to theory and research concerned with interactions between individuals, organizations, and social structures. The journal especially seeks articles dealing with topics such as the promotion of mental health, early detection and prevention of behavior disorders, effectiveness of mental health consultations, new techniques for the delivery of psychological services, and the creation of social environments that facilitate human growth and development. The journal is published quarterly in association with the Division of Community Psychology of the American Psychological Association by the Plenum Publishing Corporation, 227 West 17 Street, New York, New York 10011.

AMERICAN JOURNAL OF MENTAL DEFICIENCY

The *American Journal of Mental Deficiency* contains original articles extending our knowledge of mental retardation. The journal is published bimonthly by the American Association on Mental Deficiency at the Boyd Printing Company, 49 Sheridan Avenue, Albany, New York 12210.

AMERICAN JOURNAL OF PSYCHOLOGY

The *American Journal of Psychology* contains original research articles dealing with problems in experimental psychology. It also contains notes, discussions, and book reviews. The journal is published quarterly by the University of Illinois Press, Urbana, Illinois 61801.

AMERICAN PSYCHOLOGIST

The *American Psychologist* is the official journal of the American Psychological Association. It contains archival documents relating to business of the APA, and also publishes theoretical, empirical, and practical articles of interest to a broad spectrum of psychologists. The journal is published monthly by the American Psychological Association, 1200 Seventeenth Street, N. W., Washington, D. C. 20036.

ANIMAL LEARNING AND BEHAVIOR

Animal Learning and Behavior contains experimental,

theoretical, and review articles in conditioning, motivation, developmental processes, social and sexual behavior, and sensory processes. Studies involving human subjects are published only if they deal with principles of learning and behavior that do not apply exclusively to humans. The journal is published quarterly by the Psychonomic Society, 1108 West 34 Street, Austin, Texas 78705.

APA MONITOR

The *APA Monitor* is a newspaper containing news stories about current developments in psychology. Additionally, it contains information about current APA activities and about legislative activity pertaining to psychology. The newspaper also carries classified advertisements that publicize job openings in the various fields of psychology. The newspaper is published monthly by the American Psychological Association, 1200 Seventeenth Street, N. W., Washington, D. C. 20036.

BEHAVIOR RESEARCH METHODS AND INSTRUMENTATION

Behavior Research Methods and Instrumentation publishes articles dealing with methods, techniques, and instrumentation in experimental psychological research. The journal also contains a section on computer technology. It is published bimonthly by the Psychonomic Society, 1108 West 34 Street, Austin, Texas 78705.

BEHAVIORAL SCIENCE

Behavioral Science publishes original articles concerning living and nonliving systems: atoms, molecules, crystals, viruses, cells, organs, organisms, groups, organizations, societies, supranational systems, ecosystems, planets, solar systems, galaxies. The journal also publishes articles on mechanical, conceptual, and abstracted systems. The journal is published bimonthly by the Society for General Systems Research, University of Louisville, P. O. Box 1055, Louisville, Kentucky 40201.

BEHAVIOR THERAPY

Behavior Therapy is an interdisciplinary journal devoted to original research on the theory or practice of behavior therapy or behavior modification. Occasionally, theoretical or review articles are published in addition to experimental and clinical research articles. The journal also contains critical notices of new books, tapes, and films of relevance to the behavior therapy and modification fields. The journal is published five times a year under the auspices of the Association for the Advancement of Behavior Therapy by Academic Press, 111 Fifth Avenue, New York, New York 10003.

BULLETIN OF THE PSYCHONOMIC SOCIETY

The *Bulletin of the Psychonomic Society* contains brief articles authored or sponsored by members of the Psychonomic Society. The maximum length is two published pages. The journal is published monthly by the Psychonomic Society, 1108 West 34 Street, Austin, Texas 78705.

CHILD DEVELOPMENT

Child Development reports empirical research, theoretical articles, and reviews having theoretical implications for developmental psychology. It welcomes contributions from all disciplines that bear on developmental processes. The journal is published quarterly for the Society for Research in Child

Development by the University of Chicago Press, 5801 Ellis Avenue, Chicago, Illinois 60637.

COGNITION: INTERNATIONAL JOURNAL OF COGNITIVE PSYCHOLOGY

Cognition contains theoretical and experimental papers on the study of the mind, book reviews, notes, and discussions on current trends in scientific, social, or ethical matters. The journal is published quarterly by Elsevier Sequoia S. A., P. O. Box 851, 1000 Lausanne 1, Switzerland.

COGNITIVE PSYCHOLOGY

Cognitive Psychology publishes original empirical, theoretical, and tutorial papers, methodological articles, and critical reviews in the fields of language processing, memory, perception, problem solving, and thinking. The journal accepts articles from disciplines related to psychology so long as the articles are interesting to and understandable by cognitive psychologists. The journal is published quarterly by Academic Press, 111 Fifth Avenue, New York, New York 10003.

CONTEMPORARY PSYCHOLOGY

Contemporary Psychology publishes reviews of books in psychology, and also, occasionally, of films, tapes, and other media relevant to psychology. Reviews are written by invitation, although all readers may submit brief letters pertaining to reviews that have appeared in the journal. The journal is published monthly by the American Psychological Association, 1200 Seventeenth Street, N. W., Washington, D. C. 20036.

THE COUNSELING PSYCHOLOGIST

The Counseling Psychologist contains articles on all aspects of counseling psychology. It is published quarterly by

Division 17 of the American Psychological Association, 1200 Seventeenth Street, N. W., Washington, D. C. 20036.

DEVELOPMENTAL PSYCHOLOGY

Developmental Psychology publishes empirical research dealing with all phases of growth and development. The journal is published bimonthly by the American Psychological Association, 1200 Seventeenth Street, N. W., Washington, D. C. 20036.

EDUCATIONAL AND PSYCHOLOGICAL MEASUREMENT

Educational and Psychological Measurement publishes discussions of problems in the measurement of individual differences, research on the development and use of tests and measurements, descriptions of testing programs, and miscellaneous notes pertaining to measurement. The journal is published quarterly by *Educational and Psychological Measurement,* 3121 Cheek Road, Durham, North Carolina 27704.

HUMAN BEHAVIOR

Human Behavior is a popular journal publishing articles in the social sciences that are readable by the general public. The journal is published monthly by Manson Western Corporation, 12031 Wilshire Boulevard, Los Angeles, California 90025.

INTERNATIONAL JOURNAL OF PSYCHOLOGY

The *International Journal of Psychology* publishes papers in all fields of general psychology, including perception, learning, cognitive processes, language, child psychology, and social psychology. The journal especially seeks comparisons of experimental results obtained in different countries, replications in new cultural contexts, and international discussions of theories and methods. Emphasis is on basic research and theory rather than technical and applied problems. The journal is published quarterly for the International Union of Psychological Science by Durod, 17 rue Rémy-Dumoncel, 75680 Paris Cedex 14, France.

JOURNAL OF ABNORMAL CHILD PSYCHOLOGY

The *Journal of Abnormal Child Psychology* is devoted to theory and research dealing with psychopathology in childhood and adolescence. The journal is published quarterly by the Plenum Publishing Corporation, 227 West 17 Street, New York, New York 10011.

JOURNAL OF ABNORMAL PSYCHOLOGY

The *Journal of Abnormal Psychology* publishes articles on basic theory and research in the field of abnormal behavior. It covers topics such as psychopathology, normal processes in abnormal individuals, pathological features of the behavior of normal persons, group effects on pathological processes. Experiments, case histories, and theoretical papers are all welcome. The journal is published bimonthly by the American Psychological Association, 1200 Seventeenth Street, N. W., Washington, D. C. 20036.

JOURNAL OF APPLIED BEHAVIOR ANALYSIS

The *Journal of Applied Behavior Analysis* publishes original reports of experimental research involving applications of the experimental analysis of behavior (behavioristic techniques) to problems of social importance. Also included in the journal are technical articles and discussions of issues relevant to such research. The journal is published quarterly by the Society for the Experimental Analysis of Behavior, Lawrence, Kansas 66044.

JOURNAL OF APPLIED BEHAVIORAL SCIENCE

The *Journal of Applied Behavioral Science* publishes articles that develop or test theoretical and conceptual approaches to planned change, including reports on social interventions, evaluations of attempts at social interventions, evaluations of the underlying values and biases inherent in attempts at social change. The journal is published quarterly by the NTL Institute for Applied Behavioral Science, P. O. Box 9155, Arlington, Virginia 22209.

JOURNAL OF APPLIED PSYCHOLOGY

The *Journal of Applied Psychology* publishes original articles dealing with all areas of applied psychology except clinical psychology. The orientation of the journal is primarily empirical, although a theoretical or review article may be accepted if it presents a special contribution to an applied field. Some of the applied settings covered by the journal are universities, industry, and government. The journal is published bimonthly by the American Psychological Association, 1200 Seventeenth Street, N. W., Washington, D. C. 20036.

JOURNAL OF COMPARATIVE AND PHYSIOLOGICAL PSYCHOLOGY

The *Journal of Comparative and Physiological Psychology* contains articles dealing with physiological, anatomical, chemical, and biological mechanisms and with comparative aspects of behavior. The journal is published monthly by the American Psychological Association, 1200 Seventeenth Street, N. W., Washington, D. C. 20036.

JOURNAL OF CONSULTING AND CLINICAL PSYCHOLOGY

The *Journal of Consulting and Clinical Psychology* publishes original research on techniques of diagnosis and treatment in disordered behavior, characteristics of populations of clinical interest, cross-cultural and demographic trends in behavioral disorders, and personality and personality assessment as they pertain to consulting and clinical psychology. The orientation of the journal is primarily empirical, although theoretical articles are also published from time to time. The journal is published bimonthly by the American Psychological Association, 1200 Seventeenth Street, N. W., Washington, D. C. 20036.

JOURNAL OF COUNSELING PSYCHOLOGY

The *Journal of Counseling Psychology* contains articles on theory, research, and practice concerning counseling and the activities of counselors and personnel workers. Contributions dealing with developmental aspects of counseling and with diagnostic group, remedial, and therapeutic approaches to counseling are particularly welcome. The journal publishes occasional reviews of research and of tests used by counselors. The journal is published bimonthly by the American Psychological Association, 1200 Seventeenth Street, N. W., Washington, D. C. 20036.

JOURNAL OF CROSS-CULTURAL PSYCHOLOGY

The *Journal of Cross-Cultural Psychology* deals exclusively with cross-cultural behavioral and social research. Its main concentration is on empirical reports concerning how and why if at all psychological phenomena are differentially conditioned by culture and ecology. The focus of the journal is on individual rather than societal differences. The journal is published for the Center for Cross-Cultural Research by Sage Publications, 275 South Beverley Drive, Beverley Hills, California 90212.

JOURNAL OF EDUCATIONAL PSYCHOLOGY

The *Journal of Educational Psychology* publishes original empirical and theoretical papers dealing with learning and cognition as they relate to instruction, and with the psychological development, relationships, and adjustment of individuals. Articles report findings that for the most part are obtained in various kinds of educational settings. The journal is published bimonthly by the American Psychological Association, 1200 Seventeenth Street, N. W., Washington, D.C. 20036.

JOURNAL OF THE EXPERIMENTAL ANALYSIS OF BEHAVIOR

The *Journal of the Experimental Analysis of Behavior* contains original reports of experiments and theoretical positions relevant to the behavior of individual organisms. The journal maintains a behavioristic orientation. It is published bimonthly by the Society for the Experimental Analysis of Behavior, Department of Psychology, Indiana University, Bloomington, Indiana 47401.

JOURNAL OF EXPERIMENTAL CHILD PSYCHOLOGY

The *Journal of Experimental Child Psychology* is devoted primarily to empirical research dealing with children. It also includes critical reviews, theoretical contributions, and short notes on methodological issues and innovative apparatus pertaining to child psychology. The journal is published bi-monthly by Academic Press, 111 Fifth Avenue, New York, New York 10003.

JOURNAL OF EXPERIMENTAL PSYCHOLOGY: ANIMAL BEHAVIOR PROCESSES

The *Journal of Experimental Psychology: Animal Behavior Processes* contains experimental reports of the perception, learning, motivation, and performance of infrahuman animals. Articles are expected to make a substantial contribution to general behavior theory. The journal is published quarterly by the American Psychological Association, 1200 Seventeenth Street, N. W., Washington, D. C. 20036.

JOURNAL OF EXPERIMENTAL PSYCHOLOGY: GENERAL

The *Journal of Experimental Psychology: General* contains articles in all areas of experimental psychology. This journal solicits long, integrative reports of general interest to all experimental psychologists. The journal is published quarterly by the American Psychological Association, 1200 Seventeenth Street, N. W., Washington, D. C. 20036.

JOURNAL OF EXPERIMENTAL PSYCHOLOGY: HUMAN LEARNING AND MEMORY

The *Journal of Experimental Psychology: Human Learning and Memory* contains experimental articles on acquisition, retention, and transfer in human behavior. It is published bi-monthly by the American Psychological Association, 1200 Seventeenth Street, N. W., Washington, D. C. 20036.

JOURNAL OF EXPERIMENTAL PSYCHOLOGY: HUMAN PERCEPTION AND PERFORMANCE

The *Journal of Experimental Psychology: Human Perception and Performance* is devoted to experimental reports of human information processing operations and their relation to experience and performance. The journal is published quarterly by the American Psychological Association, 1200 Seventeenth Street, N. W., Washington, D. C. 20036.

JOURNAL OF EXPERIMENTAL SOCIAL PSYCHOLOGY

The *Journal of Experimental Social Psychology* contains primarily experimental research on social interaction and phenomena. Also included are occasional theoretical papers, literature reviews, and methodological notes. The journal is published bimonthly by Academic Press, 111 Fifth Avenue, New York, New York 10003.

JOURNAL OF GENERAL PSYCHOLOGY

The *Journal of General Psychology* publishes articles in the fields of experimental, physiological, and comparative psychology. It also contains briefly reported replications, refinements, and comments on previous work. The journal is published quarterly by the Journal Press, Box 543, 2 Commercial Street, Provincetown, Massachusetts 02657.

JOURNAL OF GENETIC PSYCHOLOGY

The *Journal of Genetic Psychology* is devoted to research in developmental and clinical psychology. In addition to standard empirical reports, it includes briefly reported replications and refinements of previous work, as well as occasional book reviews. The journal is published quarterly by the Journal

Press, Box 543, 2 Commercial Street, Provincetown, Massachusetts 02657.

JOURNAL OF THE HISTORY OF THE BEHAVIORAL SCIENCES

The *Journal of the History of the Behavioral Sciences* contains articles in the history of all the behavioral sciences. The journal is published quarterly by the Clinical Psychology Publishing Company, 4 Conant Square, Brandon, Vermont 05733.

JOURNAL OF HUMANISTIC PSYCHOLOGY

The *Journal of Humanistic Psychology* publishes experiential reports, theoretical papers, personal essays, research studies, applications of humanistic psychology, humanistic analyses of contemporary culture, and occasional poems. The journal especially solicits articles on the topics of authenticity, encounter, self-actualization, self-transcendence, search for meaning, creativity, personal growth, psychological health, being-motivation, values, identity, and love. The journal is published by the Association for Humanistic Psychology, 325 Ninth Street, San Francisco, California 94103.

JOURNAL OF INDIVIDUAL PSYCHOLOGY

The *Journal of Individual Psychology* publishes theoretical, historical, and experimental articles consonant with the Individual Psychology of Alfred Adler. It also publishes book reviews and news about Adlerian psychology. The journal is published by the American Society of Adlerian Psychology, and business correspondence is addressed to Dr. H. L. Ansbacher, University of Vermont, John Dewey Hall, Burlington, Vermont 05401.

JOURNAL OF MATHEMATICAL PSYCHOLOGY

The *Journal of Mathematical Psychology* publishes original theoretical and empirical research in all areas of mathematical psychology. The journal is published bimonthly by Academic Press, 111 Fifth Avenue, New York, New York 10003.

JOURNAL OF MULTIVARIATE EXPERIMENTAL PERSONALITY AND CLINICAL PSYCHOLOGY

The *Journal of Multivariate Experimental Personality and Clinical Psychology* publishes original investigations in personality and clinical psychology that use multivariate experimentation and theory. The journal emphasizes experimental research, but contains occasional theoretical and review articles. The journal is published quarterly by the Western Institute of Multivariate Psychology, P. O. Box 554, Ashland, Oregon 97520.

JOURNAL OF PARAPSYCHOLOGY

The *Journal of Parapsychology* primarily contains original reports of experimental research in parapsychology. It also contains reviews, theoretical and methodological articles, book reviews, comments, and letters. The journal is published quarterly by the Parapsychology Press, Box 6847 College Station, Durham, North Carolina 27708.

JOURNAL OF PERSONALITY

The *Journal of Personality* publishes investigations in the field of personality. Current emphasis is on experimental studies of behavior dynamics, character structure, personality-related consistencies in cognitive processes, and the development of personality in its cultural context. The journal is published quarterly by the Duke University Press, Box 6697 College Station, Durham, North Carolina 27708.

JOURNAL OF PERSONALITY AND SOCIAL PSYCHOLOGY

The *Journal of Personality and Social Psychology* contains original research in social psychology and personality dynamics. Among the topics included are social motivation, attitudes and attitude change, social interaction, verbal and nonverbal communication processes, group behavior, person perception, conformity, and personality dynamics. The journal is published monthly by the American Psychological Association, 1200 Seventeenth Street, N. W., Washington, D. C. 20036.

JOURNAL OF PSYCHOLOGY

The *Journal of Psychology* contains articles covering all areas of psychology. It is published bimonthly by the Journal Press, Box 543, 2 Commercial Street, Provincetown, Massachusetts 02657.

JOURNAL OF RESEARCH IN PERSONALITY

The *Journal of Research in Personality* contains experimental and descriptive research in personality and related fields. Articles cover the relationship to personality of genetic, physiological, motivational, learning, perceptual, cognitive, and social processes, in both normal and abnormal humans and animals. The journal is published quarterly by Academic Press, 111 Fifth Avenue, New York, New York 10003.

JOURNAL OF SOCIAL PSYCHOLOGY

The *Journal of Social Psychology* contains studies of persons in group settings, and of culture and personality. Special attention is given to cross-cultural articles and notes, and to field research. The journal includes briefly reported replications and refinements of previous work. The journal is published bimonthly by the Journal Press, Box 543, 2 Commercial Street, Provincetown, Massachusetts 02657.

JOURNAL OF VERBAL LEARNING AND VERBAL BEHAVIOR

The *Journal of Verbal Learning and Verbal Behavior* contains original experimental, theoretical, and review papers dealing with problems of verbal learning, human memory, psycholinguistics, and related verbal processes. The journal is published bimonthly by Academic Press, 111 Fifth Avenue, New York, New York 10003.

LEARNING AND MOTIVATION

Learning and Motivation publishes original experimental and theoretical papers dealing with basic phenomena and mechanisms of learning and motivation, including papers on biological and evolutionary influences upon learning and motivational processes. Articles deal with behavior in both animals and humans. The journal is published quarterly by Academic Press, 111 Fifth Avenue, New York, New York 10003.

MEMORY AND COGNITION

Memory and Cognition contains articles covering a broad range of topics in human experimental psychology. Included in the journal are empirical, theoretical, and review papers. The journal is published bimonthly by the Psychonomic Society, 1108 West 34 Street, Austin, Texas 78705.

MENTAL RETARDATION

Mental Retardation contains research dealing with mentally subnormal and deficient persons. It is published bi-monthly by the American Association on Mental Deficiency at the Boyd Printing Company, 49 Sheridan Avenue, Albany, New York 12210.

MONOGRAPHS OF THE SOCIETY FOR RESEARCH IN CHILD DEVELOPMENT

Monographs of the Society for Research in Child Development are long articles dealing with important aspects of child development. These are articles that because of their scope and depth would not be suitable for standard journal-length presentation. The monographs are published at irregular intervals for the Society for Research in Child Development by the University of Chicago Press, 5801 Ellis Avenue, Chicago, Illinois 60637.

MULTIVARIATE BEHAVIORAL RESEARCH

Multivariate Behavioral Research publishes substantive, methodological, and theoretical articles using or dealing with multivariate statistical techniques. The journal is published quarterly by the Society of Multivariate Experimental Psychology, and business offices are at Texas Christian University, Fort Worth, Texas 76129.

ORGANIZATIONAL BEHAVIOR AND HUMAN PERFORMANCE: A JOURNAL OF FUNDAMENTAL RESEARCH AND THEORY IN APPLIED PSYCHOLOGY

Organizational Behavior and Human Performance publishes theoretical and empirical papers in all areas of human performance and organizational psychology. The journal is published bimonthly by Academic Press, 111 Fifth Avenue, New York, New York 10003.

PERCEPTION

Perception publishes experimental and theoretical reports in the fields of animal, human, and machine perception. The journal includes full experimental reports, preliminary reports, accounts of new phenomena, theoretical discussions, and descriptions of novel apparatus. The journal is published quarterly by Pion Limited, 207 Brandesbury Park, London NW2 5JN, England.

PERCEPTION AND PSYCHOPHYSICS

Perception and Psychophysics publishes experimental investigations of sensory processes, perception, and psychophysics. Reviews and theoretical articles are also sometimes accepted. Articles deal with human and occasionally animal subjects. The journal is published monthly by the Psychonomic Society, 1108 West 34 Street, Austin, Texas 78705.

PERCEPTUAL AND MOTOR SKILLS

Perceptual and Motor Skills contains articles dealing with perception and motor skills, especially as affected by experience. It also includes articles on general methodology, and reviews. The journal is published bimonthly by *Perceptual and Motor Skills,* Box 1441, Missoula, Montana 59801.

PERSONNEL PSYCHOLOGY: A JOURNAL OF APPLIED RESEARCH

Personnel Psychology contains articles reporting research methods, research results, and application of research results to the solution of personnel problems in business, industry, and government. The journal also includes occasional literature reviews. The journal is published quarterly by *Personnel Psychology,* 3121 Cheek Road, Durham, North Carolina 27704.

PHYSIOLOGICAL PSYCHOLOGY

Physiological Psychology publishes articles in physiological psychology, and in the neurosciences in general, so long as the articles are relevant to behavior. The journal contains theoretical and empirical papers, as well as reviews. The journal is published quarterly by the Psychonomic Society, 1108 West 34 Street, Austin, Texas 78705.

PROFESSIONAL PSYCHOLOGY

Professional Psychology publishes original articles on theoretical and practical issues, including articles on applications of research, standards of psychological practice, relations among professions, delivery of services, and innovative approaches to training. The journal is published quarterly by the American Psychological Association, 1200 Seventeenth Street, N. W., Washington, D. C. 20036.

PSYCHOLOGICAL BULLETIN

Psychological Bulletin contains evaluative reviews and interpretations of substantive and methodological issues in psychology. Original research is published only when it illustrates a methodological problem or issue. The journal is published bimonthly by the American Psychological Association, 1200 Seventeenth Street, N. W., Washington, D. C. 20036.

PSYCHOLOGICAL RECORD: QUARTERLY JOURNAL IN THEORETICAL AND EXPERIMENTAL PSYCHOLOGY

The *Psychological Record* contains theoretical and experimental articles and commentary on current developments in psychology. The journal is published quarterly at Kenyon College, Gambier, Ohio 43022.

PSYCHOLOGICAL REPORTS

Psychological Reports publishes experimental, theoretical, and speculative articles, comments, special reviews, and listings of new books. The orientation of the journal is toward general psychology, rather than toward any one specialty. The journal is published by *Psychological Reports,* Box 1441, Missoula, Montana 59801.

PSYCHOLOGICAL RESEARCH: AN INTERNATIONAL JOURNAL OF PERCEPTION, LEARNING, AND COMMUNICATIONS

Psychological Research contains original reports of experimental investigations in perception, learning, communication, and related areas. Preference is given to papers emphasizing theoretical implications of the research reported. The journal is published "at frequent intervals" by Springer-Verlag, New York Inc., 175 Fifth Avenue, New York, New York 10010.

PSYCHOLOGICAL REVIEW

Psychological Review publishes articles that make a theoretical contribution to any area of scientific psychology. Empirical reports, literature reviews, and methodological papers are generally not appropriate. The journal is published bimonthly by the American Psychological Association, 1200 Seventeenth Street, N. W., Washington, D. C. 20036.

PSYCHOLOGY IN THE SCHOOLS

Psychology in the Schools contains articles reporting research, opinion, practice, theory, and problems of the school psychologist. Articles are intended to emphasize implications for practitioners working in school settings. The journal is published quarterly by the Clinical Psychology Publishing Company, 4 Conant Square, Brandon, Vermont 05733.

PSYCHOLOGY TODAY

Psychology Today is a popular journal publishing articles of interest to the general public. The journal is published monthly by the Ziff-Davis Publishing Company, One Park Avenue, New York, New York 10016.

PSYCHOMETRIKA

Psychometrika contains theoretical, methodological, review, and experimental articles dealing with the application of quantitative techniques to social, behavioral, and biological research. The journal is devoted to the "development of psychology as a quantitative rational science." The journal is published quarterly by the Psychometric Society, Department of Psychology, University of Chicago, 5848 University Avenue, Chicago, Illinois 60637.

PSYCHOPHYSIOLOGY

Psychophysiology publishes experimental, theoretical, and clinical articles, as well as descriptions of new methods in psychophysiology. The journal is published bimonthly by the Society for Psychophysiological Research, Madison, Wisconsin 53711.

QUARTERLY JOURNAL OF EXPERIMENTAL PSYCHOLOGY

The *Quarterly Journal of Experimental Psychology* contains original papers on experimental work in all branches of human and animal psychology. It contains theoretical papers, experimental papers, and book reviews. The journal is published quarterly for the Experimental Psychology Society by Academic Press, 111 Fifth Avenue, New York, New York 10003.

CHAPTER 8

Standards for Evaluating the Psychology Paper

In ,this chapter, I will enumerate some of the standards I believe my colleagues and I use in evaluating the contribution to knowledge made by psychology papers. Little has been written about how psychologists evaluate a paper's contribution. Nor have psychologists passed down from one generation to another a clearly explicated spoken tradition of evaluative standards. It is therefore remarkable that psychologists find a high level of agreement in their evaluations of each others' papers. In an *Annual Review of Psychology* chapter reviewing the literature on memory and verbal learning, Tulving and Madigan (1970) noted their own remarkable agreement in evaluations of papers, and at the same time offered some keenly perceptive tongue in cheek comments regarding the state of the literature:

> In the course of preparation for this chapter, we selected a sample of 540 publications—slightly less than one half of all relevant publications that appeared during the main time-period under review here—and independently rated each paper in terms of its "contribution to knowledge." We agreed to a remarkable extent in classifying all papers into three categories. The first, containing approximately two thirds of all papers, could be labeled "utterly inconsequential." The primary function these papers serve is giving something to do to people who count papers instead of reading them. Fu-

ture research and understanding of verbal learning and memory would not be affected at all if none of the papers in this category had seen the light of day.

The second category, containing approximately one quarter of all the papers in our test sample, fell into the "run-of-the-mill" category. These represent technically competent variations on well-known themes. Their main purpose lies in providing redundancy and assurance to those readers whose faith in the orderliness of nature with respect to ecphoric [learning and memory] processes needs strengthening. Like the papers in the first category, these articles also do not add anything really new to knowledge, and they, too, will have fallen into oblivion 10 years from now.

Many papers in the first two categories simply demonstrate again something that is already well known. Many others offer one or more of the following conclusions: (a) variable X has an effect on variable Y; (b) the findings do not appear to be entirely inconsistent with the ABC theory; (c) the findings suggest a need for revising the ABC theory (although no inkling is provided as to how); (d) processes under study are extremely complex and cannot be readily understood; (e) the experiment clearly demonstrates the need for further research on this problem; (f) the experiment shows that the method used is useful for doing experiments of this type; (g) the results do not support the hypothesis, but the experiment now appears to be an inadequate test of it. Apart from providing dull reading, papers with such conclusions share another feature: they contain an implicit promise of more along the same lines in the future. They make one wish that at least some writers, faced with the decision of whether to publish or perish, should have seriously considered the latter alternative.

The third category of papers in our sample, comprising less than 10 per cent of the total, was classified as "worthwhile," including a small group of real gems. The papers in this category carry the burden of continuous progress in our field, by clarifying existing problems, opening up new areas of investigation, and providing titillating glimpses into the unknown.

In most cases, the contribution that each particular paper makes is of necessity most modest. Nevertheless, the papers in this category unmistakably stand out from the large mass of other publications.[1] (pp. 441–442)

Most psychologists would view the literature on memory and learning (*circa* 1970) less dismally than did Tulving and Madigan. The difference in opinion, however, would more likely reflect lesser severity in applying standards than disagreement over what standards to apply. In the next section of this chapter, I will present synopses of three real papers and one imaginary paper. The three real papers are considered by many psychologists to be classics in the field of psychology. As you read the synopses, try to pinpoint the characteristics of these papers that make them classics. The imaginary paper is a prime contender for Tulving and Madigan's first category of "utterly inconsequential" papers. This paper should lack the characteristics you observed in the first three papers. In the third section of the chapter, I will present eight standards that I believe separate truly important papers from other papers, and will discuss how these standards apply to the four papers synopsized below.

Synopses of Four Psychology Papers

A CLASSIC LITERATURE REVIEW: MILLER (1956)

George Miller's (1956) "The Magical Number Seven, Plus or Minus Two: Some Limits on our Capacity for Processing Information" is undoubtedly one of the most influential and

1. Reproduced, with permission, from "Memory and Verbal Learning" by E. Tulving and S. A. Madigan, *Annual Review of Psychology,* Volume 21. Copyright © 1970 by Annual Reviews, Inc. All rights reserved.

often cited literature reviews ever published in a psychological journal. Miller opens the paper with a confession:

> My problem is that I have been persecuted by an integer. For seven years this number has followed me around, has intruded in my most private data, and has assaulted me from the pages of our most public journals. This number assumes a variety of disguises, being sometimes a little larger and sometimes a little smaller than usual, but never changing so much as to be unrecognizable. The persistence with which this number plagues me is far more than a random accident. There is, to quote a famous senator, a design behind it, some pattern governing its appearances. Either there really is something unusual about the number or else I am suffering from delusions of persecution. (p. 81)

The remainder of the paper is devoted to a case history of the persecution. This case history is summarized in the following pages.

Span of absolute judgments. In experiments on absolute judgment, subjects are asked to assign a number to represent the amount of some attribute or attributes possessed by a stimulus. Consider some examples of such experiments.

Pollack (1952) had subjects assign numbers to tones of different pitch. The pitches ranged in frequency from 100 to 8000 cycles per second, and were equally spaced along a logarithmic scale of frequencies. The experimenter varied the number of tones among which subjects had to distinguish. The number of alternative tones ranged from 2 to 14. As you would expect, subjects had little difficulty distinguishing between two tones, and a lot of difficulty distinguishing among 14 tones. The main result of interest, however, was that subjects' discrimination failed to increase beyond six different pitches. Whereas subjects were able to discriminate six different pitches with virtually no errors, they were unable consistently to discriminate more than six different pitches. This result replicated when the range of pitches was changed by a factor of about 20, and when the spacing of tones was varied.

Garner (1953) studied absolute judgments of loudness. He spaced his tones over the intensity range from 15 to 110 decibels, and used conditions with 4, 5, 6, 7, 10, and 20 different intensities. He found that the maximum number of stimulus intensities subjects are able to judge without error is about five.

Beebe-Center, Rogers, and O'Connell (1955) studied taste intensities in a similar fashion. The stimuli in their experiment were varying concentrations of salt solution. They found that subjects were able to distinguish among about four different concentrations.

Hake and Garner (1951) had subjects judge the position of a pointer in an interval along a line. Subjects were thus required to divide up the line into subjective intervals. The experimenters presented stimuli at either 5, 10, 20, or 50 different positions along the line. In one condition, subjects were told to use the numbers from 0 to 100 in making their absolute judgments. In a second condition, subjects were told to use the same number of responses as there were different stimuli (5, 10, 20, or 50). Regardless of the rating scale, subjects were found able to distinguish about 10 different positions along the line.

In other experiments, subjects have been found to distinguish about five different categories for hue, and six categories for brightness. When vibrators are placed along a subject's chest, the subject is able to distinguish about four different intensities of vibration, five different durations, and seven different locations.

Miller presents further data corroborating the basic pattern of findings described above: As measured by absolute judgments of unidimensional stimuli, subjects' limitations on processing of information (often called *channel capacity*) range over a remarkably small interval. This interval seems to be about seven plus or minus two categories, regardless of *(a)* sensory modality, *(b)* type of stimuli within modality, or *(c)* range of stimuli within modality.

Span of attention. Suppose a random pattern of dots is flashed on a screen for a very brief amount of time. How many dots can a subject report without making errors? Kaufman, Lord, Reese, and Volkmann (1949) did this experiment, flashing from 1 to 200 dots on a screen for a period of .2 second. The subject was required to report the number of dots appearing on the screen. The authors found that subjects made practically no mistakes in reporting patterns containing as many as five or six dots. Beyond this number of dots, however, subjects made frequent errors. The span of attention for random dot patterns, therefore, also seems to fall into the seven plus or minus two range.

Span of immediate memory. Suppose you are presented with a sequence of random numbers, which you are asked to recall immediately upon completion of presentation. Most people are able to recall about seven digits without error. The same limit applies to random sequences of letters or words.

Limitations on seven plus or minus two. The spans of absolute judgment, attention, and memory all seem to be about seven plus or minus two. Yet, we know from everyday experience that we are able to distinguish among more than seven faces, words, numbers, letters, etc. Hence, our limitation to seven categories would itself seem to be limited. How do we increase our ability to distinguish among stimuli? There seem to be three important ways.

First, we can make relative rather than absolute judgments. For example, suppose that we were presented with successive pairs of tone frequencies, and were asked to judge which tone in each pair was higher in pitch. We easily would be able to distinguish more than seven distinct tone frequencies. Or suppose that subjects were asked to judge which of two markers on a line was further to the right. We then could distinguish even all 50 different placements of markers in Hake and Garner's experiment. By making relative judgments, we can distinguish far more than seven categories.

Second, we can increase the number of dimensions along which the stimuli differ. In the experiments described above on spans of absolute judgment, attention, and immediate memory, all the stimuli varied along only a single dimension. In everyday life, however, most stimuli vary along multiple dimensions. For example, discrimination among tones can be increased if pitch and loudness are varied simultaneously. If two perpendicular lines were used rather than just a single one, we could distinguish more than ten different positions in the plane formed by the two lines. If the random dot patterns of Kaufman et al. (1949) were replaced with dots systematically arranged into a five-by-five square, we would have no trouble counting 25 dots. In each case, multidimensionality increases our capacity to make differentiations among stimuli.

Third, we can arrange the task so that subjects are required to make several absolute judgments in a row. Instead of presenting a single stimulus to the subject and asking him to make an absolute judgment, we present several stimuli in rapid succession, and then ask the subject to make an absolute judgment. For example, we might present several markers in rapid succession on a line, and then ask the subject to give an absolute judgment for any one of them. He is now presented with a context for the absolute judgment that was missing in the Hake and Garner (1951) experiment.

Recoding.   Under what circumstances are we limited to seven plus or minus two categories, and under what circumstances are we not so limited? Consideration of the following situations may help elucidate the limiting circumstances:

(1) People usually can repeat back only about nine binary digits (0 or 1) presented in a sequence for memorization. Thus, they will probably be able to recall *001011010* after some practice in memorizing such sequences, but they probably won't be able to repeat back *001011010010110*. Under a special set of circumstances, however, a person can repeat back as many as 40 binary digits. This set of circumstances involves recoding binary digits into larger chains. In an octal (8-digit) recoding scheme, the subject thoroughly learns the following conversion table:

$$000 = 0 \qquad 010 = 2 \qquad 100 = 4 \qquad 110 = 6$$
$$001 = 1 \qquad 011 = 3 \qquad 101 = 5 \qquad 111 = 7$$

Note that a string of three binary digits now has been recoded into a single octal digit. The subject masters this scheme, and is then presented with a long string of binary digits. Every time he or she hears a consecutive triplet of digits, he or she converts it into a single octal digit. In reciting back the digits, he or she decodes the recalled octal digit back into a string of three binary digits. If the subject previously could have remembered 10 binary digits, he or she now can remember about 30 such digits, since he or she has recoded them into groups of three.

(2) When a telegraph operator first learns Morse Code, he or she perceives each *dit* and *dah* as a separate chunk, treating it in the same way that the naive subject treats a binary digit. As the telegraph operator learns to group *dits* and *dahs* into letters, however, his or her recall improves dramatically, reaching about the same level as for letters.

(3) When you are asked to recall an English sentence, you

have no trouble recalling more than seven plus or minus two letters. You probably also can recall with little difficulty more than seven syllables or even words. Suppose, however, that you are asked to recall a sentence presented in a foreign language with which you are unfamiliar. You may be able to recall more than seven plus or minus two letters, but perhaps not more than seven plus or minus two syllables or words.

The above examples make clear the importance of the unit of encoding in assessing how much is judged, attended to, or remembered. By recoding stimuli into hierarchically organized higher-order units, we can process large amounts of stimulus information. The processing limit of seven plus or minus two applies not to any unit, but only to the highest-order unit used to encode a stimulus. Given that restriction, the processing limit is general to a wide variety of task domains, as Miller (1956) has amply shown.

> And finally, what about the magical number seven? What about the seven wonders of the world, the seven seas, the seven deadly sins, the seven daughters of Atlas in the Pleiades, the seven ages of man, the seven levels of hell, the seven primary colors, the seven notes of the musical scale, and the seven days of the week? What about the seven-point rating scale, the seven categories for absolute judgment, the seven objects in the span of attention, and the seven digits in the span of immediate memory? For the present I propose to withhold judgment. Perhaps there is something deep and profound behind all these sevens, something just calling out for us to discover it. But I suspect that it is only a pernicious, Pythagorean coincidence. (p.96)

AN EXPERIMENTAL INVESTIGATION OF FORCED COMPLIANCE: FESTINGER AND CARLSMITH (1959)

One of the most influential papers ever published in the field of social psychology was Festinger and Carlsmith's (1959)

"Cognitive Consequences of Forced Compliance." The paper investigates what happens when someone is forced to do or say something contrary to his or her own privately held opinions. Two theoretical positions had been advanced, each proposing a different outcome.

According to Janis and King (1954), opinion change will increase as a function of mental rehearsal of the previously disputed opinion. The best way to induce opinion change in a subject is to force him or her to think up and rehearse new arguments supporting the disputed opinion. Janis and King's research seemed to support this position. Subjects forced to improvise a speech supporting an opinion contrary to their own showed more change in favor of this opinion than (a) subjects merely hearing a speech advocating the disputed opinion, (b) subjects delivering a speech prepared by someone else and advocating the disputed opinion.

A different prediction was made by the theory of Festinger (1957). According to Festinger's theory, opinion change will be maximized if the pressure used to produce opinion change is just sufficient to produce the change. As the amount of pressure increases over the just sufficient amount, the amount of change toward the new opinion will decrease.

Festinger and Carlsmith's experiment was designed to distinguish between the two theories presented above. The basic idea was simple (although the execution of the experiment, described below, was rather involved). Three groups of subjects participated in an excruciatingly boring experiment. Each subject in one group was paid $1 to convince a naive subject that the experiment, in which the naive subject was about to participate, was interesting and enjoyable. Each subject in a second group was paid $20 to tell the same lie. After they had made the persuasion attempt, subjects in each of the two groups were asked to report on how interesting and enjoyable they had found the experiment. Subjects in the third (control) group were asked only to report on the experiment, not to persuade anyone that the experiment was interesting and enjoyable. According to Janis and King's theory, reports from subjects paid $20 to lie about the experiment should have been more favorable to the experiment than reports from subjects paid $1, if one assumes that the $20-subjects felt more rewarded for doing the task and therefore rehearsed more favorable thoughts about it. According to Festinger's theory, reports from subjects paid $1 to lie about the experiment should have been more favorable, since $1 provided only a minimally adequate incentive to lie. Both theories predict more favorable reports from subjects in these experimental groups than from subjects in the control group. Let us now see how the experiment was executed, and how it turned out.

Method. Seventy-one male students in the introductory psychology course at Stanford University participated in an experiment on "Measures of Performance." The subjects were presented with two tasks chosen to be as boring and monotonous as possible. In the first task, each subject was told to put 12 spools onto a tray, then to empty the tray, then to refill the tray with the 12 spools, and so on. He continued in this task for one-half hour. In the second task, each subject was presented with a board containing 48 square pegs. The subject's task was to turn each peg a quarter turn clockwise, then to turn each peg again a quarter turn clockwise, and so on. Again, the task lasted one-half hour. In both tasks, the subject was told to use just one hand and to work at his own speed. While the subject engaged in the task, the experimenter appeared to be taking notes on the subject's performance.

After the subject had completed the second task, the experimeter presented him with a spurious debriefing: He told each subject that there were two groups in the experiment. In one group, the subject's own, subjects simply came into the room and performed the tasks. In the other group, subjects were told before the experiment by a confederate of the experimenter that the tasks they were about to perform were fun, enjoyable, interesting, intriguing, and exciting.

At this point in the experiment, treatments for the control and experimental groups diverged. Subjects in the control group were asked to rate, among other things, how interesting and enjoyable the experiment had been. Subjects in the experimental ($1 and $20) groups were given further spurious information about the experiment. These subjects were told that unfortunately, the confederate was unable to appear that day because of another important commitment. This left the experimenter in the predicament of having a subject in the "second group" waiting outside, but no one to tell him how enjoyable the experiment was. The experimenter then hit upon an idea that could relieve him of his predicament. Perhaps, he suggested, the subject would be willing to volunteer to be the confederate who would tell the new subject about the experiment. If the subject would be willing to do this, the experimenter would pay him for his services, and also for possible future services as the confederate. The subject was then told either that he would be paid $1 or $20, depending upon which experimental group he was in. After agreeing to tell the lie, the subject was introduced to the new, "naive" subject, who was in fact a confederate of the experimenter who had no intention of participating in the boring experiment. Her only job was to pretend to be a new, naive subject. After lying to this confederate about the experiment, the subject was taken to another room, and was asked to rate how interesting and enjoyable the experiment had been.

The rating of the experiment by the subject completed the experiment for all subjects, regardless of group membership. After making this rating (and some others as well), the subject was given a true debriefing about the purpose and execution of the experiment.

Results. The results of the experiment supported Festinger's theory. Ratings of the enjoyableness of the experimental tasks were expressed on a −5 to +5 scale. The mean rating was −.45 in the control group, +1.35 in the $1-group, and −.05 in the $20-group. The mean rating for the $1-group differed significantly from the mean ratings for both of the other groups: These subjects found the experiment more enjoyable than did subjects in either of the other groups. The mean rating for the $20-group did not differ significantly from the mean rating for the control group, although the difference was of course in the predicted direction. Festinger and Carlsmith (1959) drew two major conclusions from these results:

> *(1)* "If a person is induced to do or say something which is contrary to his private opinion, there will be a tendency for him to change his opinion so as to bring it into correspondence with what he has done or said."
> *(2)* "The larger the pressure used to elicit the overt behavior (beyond the minimum needed to elicit it) the weaker will be the above-mentioned tendency." (pp. 209–210)

AN EXPERIMENTAL INVESTIGATION OF ORGANIZATION IN MEMORY: TULVING (1966)

Suppose that an experimenter reads to you the following list of words: *dog, carriage, license, clock, light, notion, apple, sojourn, branch, lecture, aluminum, happiness*. After completing the list, the experimenter asks you to recite back to him in any order the list of words. Suppose, though, that after you have recited back the words, the experimenter reads you the list again, with the words in a different order. He then asks you to recall the list again, reciting back as many words as you can in any order. The chances are excellent that you will recall more words on this second trial than you did on the first.

It is a well-known fact of learning theory that rehearsal of words in a list improves recall of those words over successive trials in a free-recall experiment. Learning theorists disagree, however, over as simple a matter as why recall improves over trials.

For many years, the predominant viewpoint was that of *frequency theory*. According to this theory, each time a person hears a word, the memory trace for that word is strengthened. The stronger the memory trace, the more likely a word is to be recalled. Hence, repetitions of a word will increase recall of that word as a function of the frequency with which the word is repeated.

An alternative point of view is based upon Miller's (1956) notions of recoding and unitization. This viewpoint is called *organization theory*. According to this theory, subjects hearing words in a list recode the words into higher-order subjective memory units. As subjects receive more trials on a list of words, the size of the subjective units increases. In recalling a list of words, subjects never remember more than about seven plus or minus two subjective units. Since the size of these units increases with rehearsal, however, the number of words recalled over trials increases. According to this theory, then, higher-order subjective organization rather than frequency of repetition determines increases in level of recall. Tulving's (1966) experiment was designed to distinguish between conflicting predictions of these two theories. In particular, Tulving's experiment was intended to show that greater frequency of repetition can actually reduce recall of words if the repetition somehow disrupts subjects' organization of higher-order units.

Method.   All subjects in Tulving's experiment were presented with an initial list of 18 words. They were given eight trials of free-recall learning in which to learn as much of the list as possible. Subjects then received one of two treatments. Subjects in a control group received a second list composed of 36 new words, none of which had appeared on the first list. Subjects in an experimental group received a second list composed of 18 old words (all of them from the original list) plus 18 new words (none of them from the original list). Subjects in both groups received eight trials in which to learn as much of the second list as possible

The design of the experiment can be summarized in the following way:

	FIRST LIST	SECOND LIST
Control Group	A	BC
Experimental Group	A	AB

All subjects receive the same list, A, as the first list. Subjects receive different second lists, however. Subjects in the control group receive a second list composed of two new sub-lists, B and C. Subjects in the experimental group receive a second list composed of one old sublist, A, and one new sub-list, B. Subjects were not told about the structure of the lists or the way in which they were related.

Frequency and organization theories make different predictions regarding performance on the second list. According to frequency theory, performance on the second list should be superior if one has had prior exposure to part of the list's contents. Hence, experimental group subjects should learn the list faster than control group subjects, and should show higher recall after the eight trials are completed. According to organization theory, however, learning of the second list by experimental subjects should be retarded, and final performance in the experimental group should be inferior to that in the control group. The reason for this prediction is that according to organization theory, the higher-order units formed during first-list learning may have been appropriate for that list, but they will probably be inappropriate for second-list learning. These units for the first list will thus interfere with the formation of new units for the second list. The overlap in words, and hence in subjective units, will thus hinder rather than facilitate second-list recall.

Results. The results of the experiment supported the prediction of organization theory. Subjects in the experimental group (receiving overlapping lists) showed slower learning and poorer final recall than did subjects in the control group (receiving nonoverlapping lists). The identical result was obtained when Tulving replicated the experiment with different subjects and with lists half as long as those used in this experiment. These data supplied a strong disconfirmation of a basic tenet of frequency theory—that recall increases with increased frequency of repetition.

AN IMAGINARY EXPERIMENT ON PERSON PERCEPTION

Dymond (1949, 1950) developed a scale measuring empathic ability, i.e., the ability to make accurate judgments about others. She found that the scale was successful in predicting which persons were more accurate in their interpersonal assessments. She also found that higher empathy scores were associated with higher performance IQs on the Wechsler-Bellevue Adult Intelligence Scale. It is this result that forms the basis for the imaginary experiment described below.

McDumbo, an obscure and deservedly unknown researcher, observed that the relation between Wechsler-Bellevue Performance IQ and empathy scores might be due to either of two factors. On the one hand, it might represent a genuine relation between Performance IQ and empathy. On the other hand, it might be an artifact attributable to the greater dexterity required to receive higher scores on the Wechsler-Bellevue test. According to this latter hypothesis, the true relation is between manual dexterity and empathy, not between intelligence and empathy. The results are certainly consistent with either hypothesis.

In order to investigate this hypothesis, McDumbo administered the empathy test to two groups of subjects. Subjects in one group received the Wechsler-Bellevue Performance Scale in addition to the empathy test. Subjects in the other group received homemade pencil-and-paper tests closely resembling the Wechsler-Bellevue Performance Scale, but requiring no physical manipulation of objects. If intelligence is responsible for the previously discovered relation between Wechsler-Bellevue and empathy scores, then the association should appear in scores for both groups. If, on the other hand, manual dexterity is responsible, only the Wechsler-Bellevue group should show a significant association between the ability and empathy tests.

The results of the experiment were ambiguous. Both the pencil-and-paper tests and the Wechsler-Bellevue Performance Scale showed significant associations with the empathy scale, but the degree of association for the pencil-and-paper tests was significantly less than that for the Wechsler-Bellevue. McDumbo therefore concluded that both intelligence and manual dexterity are important components of empathy.

Eight Standards for Evaluating the Contribution to Knowledge of Psychology Papers

Standard #1: *The paper contains one or more surprising results that nevertheless make sense in some theoretical context.* The papers of Miller, Festinger and Carlsmith, and Tulving all contain surprising, counterintuitive results that make sense when viewed in a new theoretical context. The surprise in Miller's paper is the omnipresence of the number seven (plus or minus two) in a wide variety of tasks measuring human information-processing capacity. This result suggests some inherent limit on our capacity to process information of any kind.

In Festinger and Carlsmith's experiment, it is surprising to find that subjects paid $1 to lie about a boring experiment later feel more positively toward the experiment than do subjects paid $20. Common sense and reinforcement theory both would predict the opposite result. But the result makes sense in terms of Festinger's *dissonance theory*. Subjects who were paid $20 can justify their lie to themselves with little difficulty: They lied for the money. Subjects paid $1, though, can scarcely justify their lie on the basis of the money received. Hence, they convince themselves that they said the experiment was interesting because it *was* interesting.

In Tulving's experiment, the surprising result is that subjects who have already memorized half the words on a list they are about to learn actually learn the new list slower than do subjects who have memorized none of the words on the new list. Common sense and frequency theory would predict the opposite result. The result makes sense, however, when viewed in the context of organization theory: The old organization is nonoptimal for the new list, and decreases rate of learning by impeding the formation of new organizational units.

McDumbo's experiment contains no surprises. Since it had been shown previously that the Wechsler-Bellevue Performance Scale correlates with the empathy measure, the replication merely confirms this result. Since the pencil-and-paper tests measure about the same thing as the Wechsler-Bellevue, it also is unsurprising that these tests correlate significantly with the empathy scale. And since these homemade pencil-and-paper tests probably are inferior to the Wechsler-Bellevue as measuring instruments, it is not surprising that they show lower correlations with other variables, including the empathy scale.

Standard #2: *The results presented in the paper are of major theoretical or practical significance.* The first three papers all contain results of major theoretical and practical significance. Miller's results suggest that humans actually have a very small capacity for processing isolated bits of information. They also show, however, that this capacity can be increased manyfold by recoding lower-order information into higher-order units. In Miller's terminology, the number of chunks of information that can be processed remains constant (at about seven), but the amount of information per chunk increases. Thus, although we can recall only about seven isolated letters, we can recall far more letters if they are chunked into words or sentences.

Festinger and Carlsmith's findings are of theoretical significance because they suggest the superiority of dissonance theory over reinforcement theory in accounting for effects of forced compliance on private opinions. The practical significance of these results is obvious. In order to persuade someone to adopt your point of view privately, you should not give them the greatest possible reward. Rather, you should give them the minimum possible reward that will entice them to adopt your viewpoint publicly.

Tulving's findings are of theoretical importance because they suggest that simple frequency principles are inadequate to explain the effect of repetition in learning. Organizational principles seem to be needed as well as or instead of frequency principles. The findings are of practical importance because they show the importance of organizing in an effective way the material to be learned. Mere rote drill is a poor way to learn material, and an ineffective organization of material can actually impede learning.

McDumbo's experiment contains no results of major

theoretical or practical importance. McDumbo presents no theory as to why empathy and performance IQ should be associated, although presumably a *post hoc* theory could be invented. The association is of some practical interest, but seems unlikely to be applied to real-world settings: People are not likely to judge emphatic ability on the basis of intelligence test scores.

Standard #3: *The ideas in the paper are new and exciting, perhaps presenting a new way of looking at an old problem.* The first three papers all deal with old problems. Miller's paper reviews the literatures on absolute judgment, attention span, and memory span. Festinger and Carlsmith study forced compliance, a standard topic of investigation in social psychology. Tulving's paper investigates the effects of repetition on learning, probably the oldest and most basic problem in the field of learning. Each paper brings to an old problem a new perspective that seems to provide a better account of basic psychological phenomena than do old perspectives. McDumbo's paper contains no new or exciting ideas—indeed, it contains scarcely any ideas at all. It reports some empirical phenomena, and provides an unconvincing explanation of these phenomena.

Standard #4: *The interpretation of results is unambiguous.* Lack of ambiguity is a standard that can be approached but not attained. When each of the first three papers was published, its impact was heightened by the seeming unambiguity in interpretation permitted by the results: The results seemed to demand the interpretation given to them. Nevertheless, the concept of a "crucial experiment"—an experiment that decides conclusively between two or more competing theories—is a myth. The experiments reviewed or reported in these papers proved to be no exceptions. Information theory, upon which Miller's article is based, has all but faded from the psychological scene. Bem (1967) has shown that Festinger and Carlsmith's result can be explained by self-perception theory as well as by dissonance theory. Sternberg and Bower (1972) have demonstrated that Tulving's result and others that followed it are more compatible with list-discrimination theory than with organization theory.

The level of ambiguity in the first three papers can be contrasted with the level of ambiguity in the fourth paper. Many years passed before these first three papers were shown amenable to persuasive alternative explanations, and in each case, the alternative explanation is nontrivial. In the case of McDumbo's paper, however, several alternative explanations are immediately apparent, most of them more convincing than McDumbo's explanation. The most plausible explanation is also the most trivial. McDumbo, you will recall, concluded that both performance IQ and manual dexterity are components of empathy. A more likely interpretation of the data is that manual dexterity is unrelated to empathy. The Wechsler-Bellevue correlated higher with the empathy scale than did the pencil-and-paper tests not because of the added manual dexterity component, but because it is a more reliable and valid measure of performance IQ.

Standard #5: *The paper integrates into a new, simpler framework, data that had previously required a complex, possibly unwieldy framework.* Miller's paper best exemplifies this characteristic. Prior to publication of the paper, absolute judgment, attention, and memory generally had been viewed as separate phenomena, and had been studied more or less independently. Miller's paper suggested a way in which diverse capacities could be understood (at least to some extent) within a single, unified framework. Miller did not claim that these three capacities were a single capacity. Rather, he claimed that they were subject to the same information-processing limitations—limitations imposed by our ability to handle at one time only seven plus or minus two chunks of information.

Standard #6: *The paper contains a major debunking of previously held ideas.* Certain ideas become so deeply ingrained in our ways of thinking that we are scarcely aware that we hold these ideas. The ideas serve as unquestioned presuppositions. Festinger and Carlsmith's major finding flagrantly violated one of these unquestioned presuppositions—that a larger reinforcement for some behavior will work at least as well as a smaller one. Tulving's major finding also flagrantly violated a generally unquestioned presupposition—that repetition of elements in a to-be-learned list will result in at least as much learning as nonrepetition of those elements.

Timing is of the utmost importance in debunking a theory. Suppose that the theory to be debunked is Theory X, and the replacement theory is Theory Y. If everyone already believes in the validity of Theory Y, a paper debunking Theory X will have little impact. Such a paper will be seen as beating a dead horse. But if most people are deeply committed to Theory X, and new results are obtained that cannot be reconciled with Theory X but that are compatible with Theory Y, then the paper debunking Theory X can have a great deal of impact.

Standard #7: *The paper presents an experiment with a particularly clever paradigm or experimental manipulation.* Psychologists admire clever experimental paradigms, even if they are not theoretically motivated. That the paradigms of Festinger and Carlsmith and of Tulving were both clever and theoretically motivated made them all the more appealing. Paradigms have lives of their own, and their life span sometimes extends well beyond that of the theory that motivated them. Variants of Tulving's part-whole paradigm have continued to appear in the memory literature, even though organization theory now attracts little research.

Standard #8: *The findings or theory presented in the paper are general ones.* Miller's theory of chunking and higher-order unitization aroused widespread interest among psychologists in part because of its unusual generality: The theory seemed applicable to a wide variety of cognitive performances. Festinger's dissonance theory also attracted interest because of its generality: It seemed capable of explaining people's rationalizations in a wide variety of everyday situations. Tulving's organization theory also seemed quite general, and was applied to memory for many different kinds of material. McDumbo, on the other hand, has no theory, and his result appears to have little generality: It merely expresses a relation between two specific variables.

A paper that meets all or even some of the standards described above is likely to fall into Tulving and Madigan's "third category." The student of psychology should be aware of these standards in evaluating the papers he or she reads, although the reader can expect to meet only a small number of them—and those modestly—in his or her own writing. Whereas the standards for good writing presented earlier in this book are ones that any student can and should meet, the standards presented in this chapter are ones to be strived for. The papers that meet these standards are the ones that are remembered when most other papers are long ago forgotten.

CHAPTER 9

Submitting a Paper to a Journal

If you write a paper that you believe makes a substantial contribution to psychological knowledge, you may want to consider submitting the paper for publication. Your academic adviser or course instructor can give you advice regarding the publishability of your paper, and an appropriate choice of a journal to which to submit the paper.

Deciding upon a Journal

If you decide to submit a paper for publication, the first step you must take is to decide upon a journal to which you want to submit the paper. Seven considerations should enter your decision:

(1) *Quality.* Journals vary widely in quality. Some journals publish papers that do little more than fill up journal space; other journals publish only outstanding contributions to the literature. Better journals generally have higher rejection rates for submitted papers, so that the probability of a paper being accepted in such journals is lower. Your adviser or course instructor can help you match the quality of your paper to an appropriate journal.

(2) *Content.* All journals limit by content the kinds of papers they accept. Journal editors use either or both of two criteria in deciding upon the appropriateness of a paper's

content. The first criterion is substantive focus. What is the topic of research? The journal may accept, for example, only developmental, or cognitive, or applied papers. The second criterion is methodological focus. How was the research done? The journal may accept, for example, only experimental, or theoretical, or review papers. Chapter 7 describes the content restrictions of many psychological journals.

(3) *Readership.* Journals vary in *(a)* who reads them and in *(b)* how many people read them. Readership depends in turn upon the quality and content of each journal, and, to a lesser extent, upon the cost of the journal. Journals publish annual statements of their circulation, so that the extent of the readership can be determined by looking through recent back issues of a journal for the annual statement. The composition of the readership can be inferred by assessing quality and content, and by examining the kinds of papers in which articles from the journal are cited.

(4) *Length restrictions.* Most journals have implicit restrictions on length of submitted papers, and some journals have explicit restrictions. If the journal's editorial statement (carried in every issue of most journals) does not make any statement about length, an examination of several recent issues of the journal will indicate the range in length acceptable to the journal editor.

(5) *Publication lag.* The length of time between acceptance of an article and publication of the article is the publication lag. Journals vary in publication lags from as little as 1 month to as much as 18 months or more. In submitting an article, the author should decide how long he is willing to wait for the article to be published, keeping in mind that there will be an additional lag from the time the paper is submitted to the time the paper is either accepted or rejected.

(6) *Cost of submission.* Most journals do not charge authors for publication. Some journals do charge, however, so that even publication of a short article can cost an author several hundred dollars. The journal's editorial statement will indicate what costs, if any, are involved. The author must decide before submitting an article to such a journal whether he or she is willing and able to meet the costs of publication.

(7) *Authorship restrictions.* A small number of journals restrict in some way their potential contributors. Submission may be by invitation only, or it may be limited to individuals belonging to or sponsored by members of some organization. The journal's editorial statement will indicate whether any such restrictions apply.

Submitting the Paper

Once you have decided upon a journal, you should make certain that your paper meets the editorial requirements of the journal. In most cases, this means that the paper conforms to the APA guidelines outlined in Chapter 6. If your paper conforms to these (or other) guidelines, you are ready to send it out. Most journals require at least two copies of the paper (including the original), and you should of course keep at least one copy for yourself. Check the journal's editorial statement for the number of copies you are required to submit. Psychology papers may be submitted to only one journal at a time. You should therefore send the paper initially to your first-choice journal, keeping in mind a second and possibly a third choice in case your paper is rejected. When you send the manuscript, include a cover letter indicating your intention to submit the manuscript, and enclose any permissions that may be needed for reproduction of copyrighted material.

The Editorial Decision

Most journal editors send out the articles they receive to reviewers. Some journals have a policy of "blind reviewing." All identifying information is removed from the manuscript, and the reviewer is not informed of the author's identity. Almost all journals keep the identity of the reviewer(s) a secret from the author. Once the journal editor has received the review(s), he may make any one of five decisions:

(1) *Acceptance without revision.* The article is accepted as is, and is immediately placed into the publication queue.

(2) *Acceptance with revision.* The article is accepted contingent upon revisions, usually minor ones. The editor sends back the article and review(s), informing the author of the changes that need to be made.

(3) *Rejection with suggestions for revisions.* The article is rejected, but the editor suggests ways in which the article might be made suitable for publication in the journal. Because the article is rejected, however, the editor does not commit himself to publication of the article, even if the specified changes are made. This decision is sometimes called "rejection without prejudice."

(4) *Rejection.* The article is rejected outright. The editor makes clear in his letter to the author that the paper is not suitable for the journal.

(5) *No decision.* The editor decides not to decide upon the article. He indicates to the author that he is withholding a decision pending either additional information or the incorporation of suggestions for revision.

What are the major reasons that editors reject articles? I asked this question of Professor Allan Wagner, editor of the *Journal of Experimental Psychology: Animal Behavior*

Processes. He indicated that by far the most common reason for rejection of papers is lack of substance: The paper represents too little work; the findings do not present a sufficient advance over what is already known; the findings are insufficient to establish a real, reproducible phenomenon. Other reasons for rejection include omission of necessary experimental procedures and controls, inappropriate or inadequate data analyses, shoddy scholarship, and a failure to place the work in a proper perspective. But Dr. Wagner indicated that the primary consideration in his decisions is the substance of the work. If the work represents a genuine contribution, then he (and other editors) will often bend over backward to help the author make the paper acceptable for publication.

The Aftermath

If an article is rejected, the author can either give up on the article or else restart the editorial process by submitting the article elsewhere. If the article is accepted, the article goes into press. The author may be asked to sign over the copyright to the publisher of the journal. He may also be sent back a copyedited version of the article. This version has on it instructions to the printer, and may also have queries to the author. The copyeditor may want to know, for example, whether a certain symbol is meant to be a particular Greek letter, or whether an editorial revision is acceptable to the author. Authors almost always receive proofs of their articles. Proofs are the printed version of the article as it will appear in the journal. The author checks the proofs for typographical and other errors. If an author makes changes in the article at this point, the author is usually charged for the cost of the changes to the printer. Finally, the article is published. Most journals are willing to supply reprints to the author. Some journals charge for any reprints the author orders; others supply a certain number of free reprints, and charge for additional ones.

If, as a student, you publish an article, you are to be congratulated. You have made an original contribution to psychological knowledge and, in the spirit of scientific enterprise, you have shared it with others.

References

Beebe-Center, J. G., Rogers, M. S., & O'Connell, D. N. Transmission of information about sucrose and saline solutions through the sense of taste. *Journal of Psychology*, 1955, *39*, 157–160.

Bem, D. J. Self-perception: an alternative interpretation of cognitive dissonance phenomena. *Psychological Review*, 1967, *74*, 183–200.

Clark, H. H. Semantics and comprehension. In T. A. Sebeok (Ed.), *Current trends in linguistics* (Vol. 12): *Linguistics and adjacent arts and sciences*. The Hague: Mouton, 1974. Pp. 1291–1428.

Clark, H. H., & Chase, W. On the process of comparing sentences against pictures. *Cognitive Psychology*, 1972, *3*, 472–517.

Cooley, W. W., & Lohnes, P. R. *Multivariate data analysis*. New York: John Wiley, 1971.

Dymond, R. F. A scale for the measurement of empathic ability. *Journal of Consulting Psychology*, 1949, *13*, 127–133.

Dymond, R. G. Personality and empathy. *Journal of Consulting Psychology*, 1950, *14*, 343–350.

Festinger, L. *A theory of cognitive dissonance*. Evanston, Illinois: Row, Peterson, 1957.

Festinger, L., & Carlsmith, J. M. Cognitive consequences of forced compliance. *Journal of Abnormal and Social Psychology*, 1959, *58*, 203–211.

Fowler, H. W. *A dictionary of modern English usage* (2nd ed.). Revised by E. Gowers. New York: Oxford University Press, 1965.

Garner, W. R. An informational analysis of absolute judgments of loudness. *Journal of Experimental Psychology*, 1953, *46*, 373–380.

Hake, H. W., & Garner, W. R. The effect of presenting various numbers of discrete steps on scale reading accuracy. *Journal of Experimental Psychology*, 1951, *42*, 358–366.

Harris, J. S., & Blake, R. H. *Technical writing for social scientists*. Chicago: Nelson-Hall, 1976.

Hays, W. L. *Statistics for the social sciences* (2nd ed.). New York: Holt, Rinehart, and Winston, 1973.

Janis, I. L., & King, B. T. The influence of role-playing on opinion change. *Journal of Abnormal and Social Psychology*, 1954, *49*, 211–218.

Kaufman, E. L., Lord, M. W., Reese R. W., & Volkmann, J. The discrimination of visual number. *American Journal of Psychology*, 1949, *62*, 498–525.

Miller, G. A. The magical number seven, plus or minus two: some limits on our capacity for processing information. *Psychological Review*, 1956, *63*, 81–97.

Minium, E. W. *Statistical reasoning in psychology and education*. New York: John Wiley, 1970.

Morrison, D. F. *Multivariate statistical methods* (2nd ed.). New York: McGraw-Hill, 1976.

Piaget, J. *The origins of intelligence in children* (M. Cook, tr.). New York: International Universities Press, 1952.

Pollack, I. The information of elementary auditory displays. *Journal of the Acoustical Society of America*, 1952, *24*, 745–749.

Publication manual of the American Psychological Association (2nd ed.). Washington, D. C.: American Psychological Association, 1974.

Runyon, R. P., & Haber, A. *Fundamentals of behavioral statistics* (3rd ed.). New York: Addison-Wesley, 1976.

Sternberg, R. J., & Bower, G. H. Transfer in part-whole and whole-part free recall: a comparative evaluation of theories. *Journal of Verbal Learning and Verbal Behavior*, 1974, *13*, 1–26.

Sternberg, R. J., & Tulving, E. The measurement of subjective organization in free recall. *Psychological Bulletin*, 1977, *84*, 539–556.

Strunk, W., Jr., & White, E. B. *The elements of style* (2nd ed.). New York: Macmillan, 1972.

Tatsuoka, M. M. *Multivariate analysis: techniques for educational and psychological research*. New York: Wiley, 1971.

Tulving, E. Subjective organization and effects of repetition in multi-trial free-recall learning. *Journal of Verbal Learning and Verbal Behavior*, 1966, *5*, 193–197.

Tulving, E., & Madigan, S. A. Memory and verbal learning. In P. H. Mussen & M. R. Rosenzweig (Eds.), *Annual review of psychology* (Vol. 21). Palo Alto, California: Annual Reviews, Inc., 1970. Pp. 437–484.

Webster's new collegiate dictionary. Springfield, Massachusetts: Merriam, 1973.

Webster's third new international dictionary of the English language, unabridged. Springfield, Massachusetts: Merriam, 1971.

Winer, B. J. *Statistical principles in experimental design* (2nd ed.). New York: McGraw-Hill, 1971.

A Sample Psychology Paper

This appendix contains a sample student psychology paper. The paper was written a number of years ago by an under graduate majoring in psychology: myself. The data presented in the paper are real but previously unpublished. The paper is presented (with minor modifications) as it was actually typed, rather than as it would appear in a journal. The purpose of including the paper in this volume is to illustrate the proper format for a paper typed according to APA guidelines.

The Effects of Time Limit Cues upon

Test Means, Variances, and Reliabilities

Robert J. Sternberg

Yale University

Effects of Time

1

Abstract

Two 3-minute, 40-item multiple-choice synonyms tests were administered consecutively to 411 juniors in a suburban high school. Students were divided into three groups, labeled Groups 1, 2, and 3. Each group received successively more information about time limits. Directions for a given group were identical before each test. Under the naive condition (first test), the test mean and variance were significantly higher for Group 3 than for Group 1. Under the sophisticated condition (second test), no significant differences were observed. Alternate form reliability was significantly higher for Group 3 than for either Group 1 or Group 2. The results are discussed in terms of psychometric properties of tests and fairness of test instructions to students.

The Effects of Time Limit Cues upon
Test Means, Variances, and Reliabilities

Mental ability test directions have long followed a variety of
procedures regarding time limits. Directions for some tests, such as
those for the Ohio State University Psychological Test (Toops,
1941), impose no time limit at all. Most test directions, however, do
impose a time limit.

Directions for tests that impose time limits differ in the amount of
information they convey to subjects about time limits. Some sets of
directions, such as those for Level 5 of the Lorge-Thorndike Intelligence Tests (Lorge & Thorndike, 1957) and for the Terman-
McNemar Test of Mental Ability (Terman & McNemar, 1941), inform subjects that they will be timed, but do not specify to them just
how much time they will have. Other sets of directions, such as
those for grades 9-12 of the Henmon-Nelson Tests of Mental Ability
(Lamke & Nelson, 1957) and for the Beta Test of the Otis Quick-
Scoring Mental Ability Tests (Otis, 1954), inform subjects both of
the existence of a time limit and of what the time limit is. The Otis
directions further provide for subjects to be visually reminded of
how much time they have left to work. Examiners are instructed to

write on a blackboard the time that the test began, and they are urged to write below it the time that the test will end.

In all four of these speeded tests, subjects are informed that they will be timed. The amounts of information they are given about time limits differ, however. There seem to exist in these tests, and in others like them, two basic procedures and a variation in one of them regarding how much information subjects are given about time limits. For convenience, the two procedures and variation will be referred to as Procedures 1, 2, and 3, and subjects taking tests under these procedures will be referred to as subjects in Group 1, Group 2, and Group 3 respectively. Under Procedure 1, subjects are not told how much time they will have to work on the test. Under Procedure 2, subjects are given this information. Under Procedure 3, subjects are told how much time they will have to work and are also reminded during the test of how much time they have left to work.

This experiment was designed to investigate the effects of subjects' differential exposure to time limit cues upon means, variances, and reliabilities of tests administered under two conditions. The first (naive) condition was the administration of a first test under a particular procedure. The second (sophisticated) condition was the administration of a second form of that test under the

Effects of Time

4

same procedure immediately following the administration of the first test.

The motivation underlying this experiment is that supplying subjects with more information about time limits results in a test that is both fairer to subjects and psychometrically more sound. Subjects not given full information about time limits will not know how quickly they are expected to work, and hence will not be able to pace themselves to finish as many test items as they can. Subjects who might do quite well if they knew how much time they had may do quite poorly simply because they do not realize how quickly they need to work. These considerations led to five hypotheses regarding experimental outcomes:

1. The mean of a first test administered under Procedure 1 will be lower than that of the test administered under Procedure 2, and this mean in turn will be lower than that of the test administered under Procedure 3.

Subjects taking a first test under each of the successive procedures should be increasingly better able to employ what Millman, Bishop & Ebel (1965) call time-using strategies. Such strategies are employed by test-wise examinees in order to obtain high scores. Millman et al. (1965) note that a "rule of thumb is to determine how far one should be when a specific proportion of the testing period has elapsed" (p. 714). Periodic checks on rate of progress facilitate the maintenance of proper speed (Cook, 1957; Millman et al., 1965).

2. The means of an alternate form of the first test, when the alternate form is administered to each group immediately after and under the same procedure as the first test, will not differ significantly from each other.

The signal to stop work on the first form of the test can itself serve as a time limit cue. The less information subjects have when they take the first test, the more information this implicit cue can be expected to impart. Thus, subjects in each successive group will profit increasingly less from the cue, and test means will tend to converge.

3. The variance of a first test administered under Procedure 1 will be lower than that of the test administered under Procedure 2, and this variance in turn will be lower than that of the test administered under Procedure 3.

Subjects may differ greatly in the speeds at which they can solve test items, but the extent of the difference will be masked if subjects work at their typical rates rather than their maximum rates. Greater amounts of time limit information enable potentially rapid test takers to show how rapidly they can work.

Effects of Time

6

4. The variances of an alternate form of the first test, when the alternate form is administered to each group immediately after and under the same procedure as the first test, will not differ significantly from each other.

Because the signal to stop work on the first form of the test serves as a time limit cue telling subjects the tests are strictly timed, subjects in each group realize they must work at their maximum rate on the second test. Hence, the variances in the different groups should tend to converge.

5. If two alternate forms of a test are administered under the same procedure, one immediately following the other, the alternate form reliability of the test will be lower under Procedure 1 than under Procedure 2, and lower under Procedure 2 than under Procedure 3.

As an implicit time limit cue, the signal to stop work on the first test imparts new time limit information to subjects. The greater the amount of new information transmitted, the greater will be the potential for new variance to enter into scores on the second test. The greater the amount of new variance that enters into scores on the second test, the lower will be the correlation (alternate form reliability) between forms of the test. In other words, increasing the amount of time limit information explicitly given to subjects increases the extent to which two successive forms of the test measure the same thing.

Method

Subjects

Subjects were 411 juniors in a suburban New Jersey public high school. There were 140 students in Group 1, 148 students in Group 2, and 123 students in Group 3.

Materials

The stimulus materials were alternate forms of a 40-item multiple-choice synonyms test. Test items were ordered and forms equated according to the frequency of occurrence of the test words in the English language as reported by Thorndike & Lorge (1944).

Design

Dependent variables were the number of items correctly answered on each form of the synonyms test minus one-fourth the number of items incorrectly answered. Omissions were not counted as incorrect. Independent variables were time limit instructional

Effects of Time

8

procedure (1, 2, or 3) and test form (1 and 2). Each subject was assigned to only one instructional procedure, but all subjects received both test forms under that procedure. Homerooms (where testing took place) were randomly assigned to groups. In the high school, students are assigned to homerooms at random.

Procedure

Students were tested by their homeroom teachers preceding their daily classes. The students were given no advance notice of the tests. Instructions for each of the three groups were identical except for time limit and group coding information. Students were instructed to answer as many items as they could, but to guess on items only if they had some idea of what the correct answer was, since a percentage of the number of wrong (but not omitted) answers would be subtracted from the number of correct answers.

Students in Group 1 were told that they would be timed, but they were not told how much time they would have. Students in Group 2 were told before the beginning of each of the two tests that they would have three minutes in which to work on the particular test. Students in Group 3 were also given this information, and were further informed that they would be told when they had 2 minutes, 1 minute, and 30 seconds left to work.

After the initial instructions were completed, students in all groups received Form 1 of the synonyms test. After the test, the instructions were repeated, and then students received Form 2 of the synonyms test. Following administration of Form 2, the homeroom teacher collected the test booklets, ending the experimental session.

Results

Test means, variances, and alternate form reliabilities are presented in Table 1.

Insert Table 1 about here

Test 1 Means

The first hypothesis was partially confirmed by the results. The three group means for the first test fell into the rank order predicted, although only the difference between the first and third means was significant, $t(261) = 1.85$, $p < .05$.

Test 2 Means

The Test 2 means were consistent with the second hypothesis. None of the means differed significantly from each other.

10

Test 1 Variances

The experimental data provided a partial confirmation of the third hypothesis. Test 1 variances fell into the rank order predicted, although again, only the difference between the Group 1 and Group 3 variances was significant, $F(122,139) = 1.67$, $p < .01$.

Test 2 Variances

The Test 2 variances were consistent with the fourth hypothesis. None of the variances differed significantly from each other.

Alternate Form Reliabilities

The rank order of the alternate form reliabilities was that predicted by the fifth hypothesis. The difference between Groups 1 and 3 was significant, $z = 3.40$, $p < .01$, as was the difference between Groups 2 and 3, $z = 2.47$, $p < .01$.

Discussion

The data presented above suggest that authors of mental ability tests may have been too cavalier in determining how much time limit information should be imparted to examinees. Reduced time limit information has been shown in this experiment to result in lower test means and variances for an initial test, and to result in lower alternate form reliability. This last finding is of particular importance, since it suggests that withholding time limit information from subjects may result in a psychometrically poorer test. Telling subjects the time limit of a test and reminding them during testing of how much time is left is fairer to the subject, since it enables him to budget his time, and fairer to the tester, since it gives him a better, more consistent view of each subject's maximal performance. Given the choice, subjects opt for the additional information.[1]

It would be worthwhile to determine whether differences in test means, variances, and reliabilities hold up across different types of test content, and to determine whether differences extend to other test statistics, particularly predictive validity. An experiment investigating the generalizability of these findings is presently being prepared (Sternberg, Note 1). If the findings are generalizable, then test authors should provide an explicit rationale for the type of time limit instructions they select.

Effects of Time

12

Reference Note

1. Sternberg, R. J. Effects of time limit cues upon validity of verbal and mathematical ability test scores. Manuscript in preparation, 1971.

Effects of Time

13

References

Cook, D. L. A comparison of reading comprehension scores obtained before and after a time announcement. Journal of Educational Psychology, 1957, 48, 440–446.

Lamke, T. M., & Nelson, M. J. The Henmon-Nelson Tests of Mental Ability, Grades 9–12. Boston: Houghton Mifflin, 1957.

Lorge, I., & Thorndike, R. L. The Lorge-Thorndike Intelligence Tests, Level 5. Boston: Houghton Mifflin, 1957.

Millman, J., Bishop, H., & Ebel, R. An analysis of test-wiseness. Educational and Psychological Measurement, 1965, 25, 707–726.

Otis, A. S. Otis Quick-Scoring Mental Ability Tests, Beta Test. New York: Harcourt, Brace & World, 1954.

Terman, L. M., & McNemar, Q. Terman-McNemar Test of Mental Ability. Yonkers, New York: World Book Company, 1941.

Thorndike, E. L., & Lorge, I. The teacher's word book of 30,000 words. New York: Teachers College, Columbia University, 1944.

Toops, H. A. The Ohio State University Psychological Test. Chicago: Science Research Associates, 1941.

Effects of Time

14

Footnotes

An earlier version of this paper was submitted to Professor Leonard Doob in partial fulfillment of the 1969 requirements for Psychology 36a, Yale University. I am grateful to Dr. Doob for his comments on the paper. A version of this paper was presented at the 1972 annual meeting of the National Council on Measurement in Education, Chicago, Illinois. If this paper appeared in a journal, requests for reprints would be sent to Robert J. Sternberg, Department of Psychology, Yale University, New Haven, Connecticut 06520.

[1] An informal poll of 15 students who had participated in the experiment revealed unanimous agreement that providing greater amounts of time limit information is better for students because it enables them to budget their time more efficiently.

Table 1

Means, Variances, and Alternate Form Reliabilities

Group	Means		Variances		Reliabilities[a]
	Test 1	Test 2	Test 1	Test 2	
1	7.43	12.35	32.49	43.82	.74
2	8.10	11.64	41.47	59.75	.79
3	8.95	12.89	54.17	56.25	.88

[a]Reliabilities are of the alternate form type.

Figure Captions

Figure 1. The caption for Figure 1 would have been placed here, had there been any figures in the paper. (The figure would have followed on the next page.)

Figure 2. The caption for Figure 2 would have been placed here, had there been a second figure in the paper. (The figure would have followed Figure 1 on the page after the next.)

Writing
The Psychology Paper

INDEX

A

Abbreviations, 79, 135-136
Abstracts, 63-64
Active voice, use of, 85
Advice, seeking, 39-40, 91
Affiliation, 63
Affirmative constructions, 86
American Psychological
    Association (APA), 121, 159,
    215
Analyses of data, 13-14, 26, 43, 48,
    61-62, 70
APA (American Psychological
    Association), 121, 159, 215
Apparatus, 66
Appendices, 73-74
Arguments:
    evaluation of, 25-27
    taking notes on, 25
Articles (*see* Journal articles)
Audience, 35-36, 78, 214
Auditory directions, 54
Auditory presentations, 53
Author cards, 23-24
Author's name, 63
Autobiographical information,
    15-17, 90

B

Between-subjects variables, 46-48
Bibliography (*see* References)
Books, documentation of, 23-24
Boring topics, 20
Brackets, 130
Broad topics, 21-22

C

Capitalization, 131-133
Cards, note, 23-28
Clarity, 79
College students, as experimental
    subjects, 49, 57
Colons, 124-125
Commas, 123-124
Complicated words and sentences,
    84-85
Computer analyses, 55
Concluding sections, 28
Conclusions, 5-6, 11-13, 50
Concreteness, 84-85
Consent forms, 55-58
Consistency of arguments, 26, 37
Consistency of organization, 32-33
Constructions, 86-87

Contradictions, 26
Contributions, 7, 10, 27, 65
Control, experimental, 44
Controlled experiments, 14
Course work in psychology,
    undergraduate, 40

D

Dangling constructions, 86-87
Dashes, 126
Data:
    reporting of, 67-69
    scoring of, 54-55
Data analyses, 13-14, 26, 43, 48,
    61-62, 70
Debriefing sheets, 58-59
Dependent variables, 44-46
Design, 65, 67
Diction, 82-85
Dictionaries, 134-135
Difficult topics, 20-21
Digressions, 81
Direct quoting, 25
Directions, writing of, 54
Discussion sections, 69-73
Documentation, 23-28
    (*See also* Reference notes;
        References)

E

Easy topics, 20
Ecological validity, 44
Edited books, documentation of, 24

Emphasis, 80
Equations, 138-140
Evaluations of arguments, 25-27
Evaluations of papers, 189-218
Evidence, 5-6, 11-13, 26, 42-43
Execution of experimental research,
    60-61
Experience, personal, use of, 43
Experimental control, 44
Experimental materials, 50-54
Experimental research papers (*see*
    Research papers, experimental)
Experimental sessions, 60-61
Experimenters, detrimental effects
    of, 61
Experiments, 14-15, 26, 44, 49
    (*See also* Materials; Subjects;
        Variables)
Explanations, 5, 9

F

Facts, 5-6, 9, 11-13, 26
    (*See also* Evidence)
Faculty consultations, 39-40, 41,
    213
Failures, 11-13
Figures, 68-69, 74-75, 155-157
Footnotes, 23-24, 73-74, 148-150,
    153-154
    (*See also* Reference notes)

G

Generalizations, 48-49, 50
Grammar, 86-88, 123-136

H

Headings, 28, 136-137
HEW (U.S. Department of Health, Education, and Welfare), 55
Hierarchic organization, 34-35
Honesty, 6, 11-13
Hyphens, 125-126
Hypotheses (*see* Theories)

I

Ideas, logical development of, 13-17, 78
Ideas, for research (*see* Topics)
Implications of arguments, 27, 37
Implications of experiments, 70-71
Importance of arguments, 27, 37
Independent variables, 43-44, 46-48
Index cards, 23-28
Interest, 19-20
Internal consistency, 26, 37
Introductory sections, 28, 64-65, 77
Italics, 133-134

J

Journal articles, documentation of, 23
Journals, 15-16
  acceptance by, 8, 216-218
  basic list of, 166-187
  rejection by, 3-4, 16, 216-217
  submission to, 213-218

K

Keypunched data, 55
Keyword outlines, 28-29, 31

L

Legibility, 122-123
Length, of papers, 4, 214
Library research papers (*see* Research papers, library)
Literature, scientific:
  inadequate, 21
  mentioned in introduction, 64-65
  searching, 23-28, 40-43
  too much, 21-22
Logical development of ideas, 13-17, 78

M

Margins, 122
Materials, experimental:
  choosing, 50-53
  presenting, 53-54
  reporting on, 66
Measurement, units of, 137-138
Method sections, 66-67
Misconceptions, common, 1-17
Misused words, 93-120
Modality of direction, 54
Modality of presentation, 53-54

N

Narrow topics, 22
National Science Foundation (NSF), 55
Negative constructions, 86
Negative results, 11-13
Note cards, 23-28
Note-taking, 22-28

NSF (National Science Foundation), 55
Numbers, 140-142

O

Organization, 1-2, 74-75
  (*See also* Steps in writing)
Organization, of outlines, 31-36
Original ideas, 7
Outlines, 28-36, 62
  advantages, 36
  organization, 31-36
  types, 28-31
Overexplanation, 81-82
Overreaction, 10
Overstatement, 8, 11, 27, 82

P

Pagination, 75, 122
Paper, 121
Paraphrasing, 25
Parentheses, 129-130
Persuasion, 6-7
Phenomena, 13
Pilot subjects, testing, 59-60
Point of view, 5-6, 25, 26, 34
Population, and subject selection, 48-49, 51
Precise words, 84
Presentation, of experimental materials, 53-54
Presuppositions of arguments, 26-27, 37
Procedure, 67
Procrastination, 19

Proof, methods of:
  direct, 10-11
  indirect, 8-10
Proofreading, 90-91
Psychological Abstracts, 63
Psychology courses, undergraduate, 40
Publication lag, 214
Publication Manual of the American Psychological Association, 121
Punctuation, 123-130
Purpose, of scientific writing, 5-8, 20

Q

Qualifiers, 82-83
Quantitative issues, 137-143
Quotation marks, 126-129
Quoting direct, 25

R

Random sampling, 49
Reading (*see* Literature, scientific)
Redundancy, 79-81
Reference notes, 23-24, 73-74
  final listing, 147-148
  in text, 146-147
  (*See also* Footnotes)
References:
  basic, 159-187
  consulting, 40-41
  final listing, 73, 145-146
  initial compilation, 22, 23-24
  in text, 143-145
Refutation, 8-11, 13

Reporting experimental research, 62-75
Research, planning:
    choosing materials, 50-53
    choosing means of presentation, 53-54
    consent forms, 55-58
    debriefing sheets, 58-59
    getting an idea, 39-43
    how data will be analyzed, 48
    scoring data, 54-55
    selecting dependent variables, 44-46
    selecting independent variables, 43-44
    selecting subjects, 48-50
    testing subjects, 59-60
    types of variables, 46-48
    writing directions, 54
Research papers, experimental, 39-75
    analyzing data, 61-62
    executing research, 60-61
    planning research, 39-60
    reporting on research, 62-75
Research papers, library, 19-37
    deciding on a topic, 19-23
    preparing an outline, 28-36
    selecting the literature, 23-28
    writing the paper, 36-37
Response sheets, 54-55
Results sections, 67-69, 71-73
Rules, for writing, 77-91

S

Safe topics, 20

Sampling procedures, 49, 51
Scientific literature (see Literature, scientific)
Semicolons, 124
Sentence outlines, 30, 31
Sentences, 85
Seriation, 142-143
Simpler words and sentences, 84-85
Spacing, 122
Spelling, 134-135
Standards, 189-218
Statistics, 67-68, 78, 138
Stencil keys, 55
Steps in writing:
    experimental research papers, 39-75
    library research papers, 19-37
Stratified sampling, 49
Style, 2-4, 77-91
Subjects:
    college students as, 49, 57
    and consent forms, 57-58
    and debriefing sheets, 59
    reporting on, 66-67
    selection of, 48-50
    testing pilot, 59-60
Summary statements, 89

T

Tables, 68-69, 73-74, 150-155
Technical terms, 78, 103-120
Testing pilot subjects, 59-60
Thematic organization, 33-34, 72
Theories, 26, 42-43, 50, 52
Titles, 23, 62-63, 77
Topic cards, 25-28

Topic outlines, 29-30, 31
Topics:
  deciding upon, 19-23, 39-43
  recording information about,
    25-28
  relevant and irrelevant, 36
Transitions, 89
Typing, 24, 121-123

U

Undergraduate psychology courses,
  40
Undergraduate research papers (*see*
  Research papers, library)
Understatement, 8, 10-11
U.S. Department of Health,
  Education, and Welfare (HEW),
  55
Usage, 93

V

Validation, 26, 37
Validity, of arguments, 25-26, 37
Validity, ecological, 44
Variables, 14, 54, 67
  between-subjects, 46-48
  dependent, 44-46
  independent, 43-44
  within-subjects, 46-48
Vehicle of presentation, 53
Visual directions, 55
Visual presentations, 53
Vocabulary, 78

W

Within-subjects variables, 46-48
Word choice, 82-85
Words, commonly misused, 93-120
Writing, in general:
  creative aspect, 1-2
  development of ideas, 13-17
  length, 4
  methods of proof, 8-11
  purpose, 5-8, 16
  style, 2-4
  use of negative results, 11-13
  (*See also* Research papers)
Writing, actual, 36-37, 62-75
Writing rules, 77-91